KARL MARX
Our Contemporary

KARL MARX
Our Contemporary
Social Theory for a Post-Leninist World

Keith Graham

University of Toronto Press
Toronto and Buffalo

First published in North America by
University of Toronto Press 1992
Toronto and Buffalo

ISBN 0–8020–2921–3 (cloth)
ISBN 0–8020–7424–3 (paper)

Printed and Bound in Great Britain
Toronto Studies in Philosophy

Canadian Cataloguing in Publication Data

Graham, Keith
  Karl Marx : our contemporary social theory for a
  post-Leninist world
  Includes bibliographical references.
  ISBN 0–8020–2921–3 (bound)
  ISBN 0–8020–7424–3 (pbk.)
  1. Philosophy, Marxist.   I. Title
  B809.8G73 1992   335.4'11   092–C94160–5

To GAC

'*Die Philosophen haben die Welt nur verschieden* interpretiert, *es kommt darauf an sie zu* verändern.' KARL MARX

'*Transcendence of custom is the most important fact in the intellectual history of mankind.*' ERNEST GELLNER

Contents

Acknowledgements

Some passages in Chapter 2 originally appeared in 'Morality, individuals and collectives', in J. D. G. Evans (ed.), *Moral Philosophy and Contemporary Problems*, Royal Institute of Philosophy Lecture Series: 22, Cambridge University Press, © The Royal Institute of Philosophy 1987; and in 'Morality and abstract individualism', *Proceedings of the Aristotelian Society*, vol. 87, © Aristotelian Society 1986/7. Chapter 4 contains material previously published in 'Class – A simple view', *Inquiry*, vol. 32, © Universitetsforlaget 1989. Chapters 4 and 5 contain some material previously published in 'Self-ownership, communism and equality', *Supplementary Proceedings of the Aristotelian Society*, vol. 64, © Aristotelian Society 1990. Such material is reprinted by courtesy of the respective editors.

I am grateful to Stephan Körner for inviting me to write a book about Marx, to Sue Cooper and Farrell Burnett for allowing me to concentrate exclusively on Marx's contemporary relevance, and for their patience in the wake of broken deadlines.

I received helpful suggestions from university audiences in Aberdeen, Bangor, Birmingham, Bradford, Essex, Exeter, Glasgow, Kent, the London School of Economics, and St Andrews; and from Alison Assiter, Richard Bellamy, Chris Bertram, Alan Carling, Alan Carter, John Cleave, Joe Femia, Martin Hollis, Bill Jordan, Andrew Mason, Adam Morton, and John O'Neill.

David Archard, John Baker, and G. A. Cohen all kindly gave me extensive comments on an entire draft, and saved me from many errors. I have had to ignore many of their astute points, for lack of space and lack of a good answer.

My greatest debt is to Cohen. At our first meeting it became apparent that we each attached a very different philosophical and political significance to Marx's writings, but he has been willing to pursue those differences with me over the course of a quarter of a century. I have learnt much from his example about the importance of honestly trying to follow the argument where it leads. The book is dedicated to him.

/one/

Introduction

As little as twenty years ago, a good excuse was necessary for writing an English philosophy book on Karl Marx. Little of his mature work had the appearance of 'conceptual analysis', and at that time political philosophy was itself fairly peripheral. Times have changed. John Rawls's *A Theory of Justice* revived political philosophy, and many other substantial works followed. Philosophical study of Marx's own writings was revolutionized by G. A. Cohen's *Karl Marx's Theory of History* (Cohen, 1978), and lengthy and intricate debates still continue on the issues he raised. Indeed, so great has been the explosion of new work on Marx that it might be doubted whether it can be significantly added to. An excuse is once more needed for writing a philosophy book about Marx, but now for the opposite reason. Why add yet more to the available stock?

Undoubtedly, however, the strongest reason for questioning the timeliness of a book about Marx would be the collapse of regimes bearing his name. They have been amongst the most brutal and oppressive of the modern age, but their time is up and the politics on which they were based have been abandoned even by their erstwhile supporters. At most, then, it might be concluded that a discussion of Marx's philosophy would resemble an examination of a diseased corpse. The only remaining question would be the cause of death.

Now either claims like this are true: either a large part of the twentieth century was given over to practical experiments in Marxism in places like Eastern Europe, China and Cuba, in which case we have ample grounds for rejecting Marx's doctrines. Or . . . Or what? That is the question I implicitly try to answer in this book.

I

1.1 Background

I present an interpretation of Marx far removed from anything which would justify the regimes in question. This continues the project of a previous book, *The Battle of Democracy* (Graham, 1986a), where I argued, in effect, the need for a *post-Leninist Marxism*. On this occasion, however, I am concerned with Marx's views at a more basic level, and the misinterpretations I wish to rescue him from are more widely held. The idea that many previous attempts to understand Marx have gone badly wrong is not as preposterous as it might seem. Ever since his death (and before it) his name has been appropriated by people with particular axes to grind. Hardly anyone comes to Marx's writings – if they come to them at all – without presuppositions about what they will find there, and in this way a kind of cumulative error becomes not merely possible but likely. Many views attributed to him have no basis in what he wrote. No one (including me) is neutral on the subject of Marx, and there is really no substitute for reading him oneself.

He published voluminously during his lifetime, and many commonly cited works were published posthumously. There is a difficulty here if we are concerned with recapturing *Marx's* thought. Personally, I should not like to be judged after my death by writings pushed to the back of a drawer, in which I might have been simply trying out ideas I was uncertain of or later came to reject. I have extended the same charity to Marx[1] and concentrated on his own output, particularly the *magnum opus*, *Capital*, vol. 1. I have tried not to rely on posthumous material except where it can be corroborated by work Marx himself published. The major exception to this is *The German Ideology* (Marx and Engels, 1932), which contains the longest exposition of the theory of history, and which Marx and Engels did try to get published in their own time (cf. McLellan, 1973: 151). The minor exception is my epigraph from the *Theses on Feuerbach* – the most potent formulation of Marx's overriding concern with *practice*, the desire to change the world. Whether published or not, Marx is stuck with this remark for some time, since it is chiselled on his tomb in Highgate cemetery.

1.2 Analytical Marxism

Many different kinds of Marx studies are worthwhile. There is the enterprise of relating his views to his social and intellectual context. Arguably, until we have done this, in a fairly literal sense we have an incomplete grasp of *what Marx was doing* in expressing the views he did.[2] There is also the enterprise of subjecting Marx's views to empirical testing, at least where they are sufficiently determinate for this to be possible. My enterprise is distinct from either of these. It will consist of taking positions which can plausibly be attributed to Marx on the basis of his texts, examining the concepts and categories they employ, and assessing the cogency of the arguments which can be put forward in their support. In this way I hope to reconstruct the philosophical basis on which Marx's claims rest.

I therefore scrutinize the most basic terms in Marx's vocabulary and the use to which he puts them. We shall see that at many points acceptance or rejection of what he has to say depends on some contentious philosophical question. That cuts both ways, of course. On the one hand, standard dismissals of Marx are too easy. Marx is our contemporary just because these questions are the subject of perennial or current debate. On the other hand, Marx's own position often cannot be established without much philosophical argument, and reaching definitive conclusions on philosophical questions is notoriously difficult.

I suggest, however, that his views are sufficiently subtle and rich, and are expressed at such a level of generality and abstraction, as to be of contemporary interest. They are not *essentially about* nineteenth-century capitalism; they are about capitalism as such, which happened to be exemplified in a particular way in his own time. It is a massive task to decide how much of his argument works once we have recognized its abstractness and then look at it in the light of the present. Whether it is accepted or not, I do at least offer a new interpretation of Marx. It may not be wholly new in an absolute sense: elements of my interpretation may have been present in the work of earlier commentators. But the picture which emerges would not normally be associated with Marx's name.

Normal principles of charitable interpretation apply. For example, it might be thought that to reconstruct the basis of Marx's theories we must conduct an exhaustive survey of all relevant passages. The volume of his writings makes this impracticable,[3] and even if it were feasible we should certainly find that Marx contradicted himself. No one could write so much and fail to do so. But this no more precludes reconstructing a consistent basis for his theories than it would, say, in the case of Hume. One fastens on the main drift of thought and tries to make sense of that. This does, of course, mean that there are many Marxes, and neither I nor anyone else can claim to have the one true interpretation. I would claim for mine that it is neglected, interesting and supportable by the texts.

Naturally, there are dangers in this exercise. Attempting to provide philosophical foundations for someone's views involves presenting their work in ways in which they did not, and providing argumentation they may not themselves have used. One recalls Karl Popper's statement, before his attack on Marx's 'historicism':

> I have not hesitated to construct arguments in [historicism's] support which have never, to my knowledge, been brought forward by historicists themselves. I hope that, in this way, I have succeeded in building up a position really worth attacking. (Popper, 1957: 3)

At least when the aim is to provide a sympathetic, rather than hostile, account there is less danger of simply setting up a straw person to shoot at.

Philosophical reconstruction of Marx's theories is necessary. It is easy to misinterpret him at a basic level, so that the more complex positions attributed to him are themselves vitiated by proceeding from ill-founded basic assumptions. Marx himself might not thank a commentator for this kind of attention, of course. He wrote in particular circumstances, often with particular objectives in mind; and even when his writing is deeply theoretical it is informed by his wish, above all, to change the world. But whether such attention would be welcome or not, it is legitimate to ask whether someone's philosophical assumptions are defensible.

An investigation of this kind is likely to be associated with the growing literature in *analytical* or *rational choice Marxism*, a body of work associated with figures such as G. A. Cohen, Jon Elster, Adam Przeworski, John Roemer and Erik Olin Wright. It is not clear to me how much homogeneity there is in their work, but my project certainly matches the features which some of them have distinguished as the essence of analytical Marxism. It involves 'the systematic interrogation and clarification of basic concepts and their reconstruction into a more coherent theoretical structure' (Wright, 1985: 2). It also involves 'abstraction' as opposed to dealing with concrete historical episodes, and a 'search for foundations' for Marx's claims (Roemer, 1986: 1).

However, I reject certain points of doctrine widely shared by analytical Marxists. In Chapter 2 I describe and criticize their commitment to various forms of individualism and their belief that the findings of rational choice theory present a major problem for Marx. In Chapter 4 I suggest that several of them employ a conception of class which is at some distance from Marx's own. Whatever doctrinal differences exist, though, the great achievement of analytical Marxism is to have shown by example that there is something in Marx worth arguing about. Crude and brutal regimes claiming the name Marxist quickly evolved crude and brutal interpretations of Marxism. Generations of neutral observers could then be forgiven for thinking that if *that* was what Marx thought, he had no place on the philosophical agenda. As a result of the efforts of analytical Marxists, it may never again be possible to take that view.

1.3 Structure of the Book

Marx does not divide his work up neatly for the benefit of those interested in its philosophical foundations. I have tried to introduce such divisions, by distinguishing:

- basic ideas about human beings;
- theses about the nature of human history in general;
- theses about the nature of his own epoch;
- practical proposals for change.

Successive chapters of the book reflect these divisions. I do not intend to imply any *derivation* from one stage to the next. There is no linear progression, any more than there is one master thesis from which all others can be deduced.

What is generally termed Marx's historical materialism, or materialist conception of history, straddles the first two divisions. In Chapter 2 I suggest that he has reasons for emphasizing the importance of material existence independently of any theses about history. This constitutes his *basic materialism*. I also call attention to the importance of collectives in his basic ontology.

In Chapter 3 I discuss his general theory of history. I introduce a distinction between his *synchronic materialism*, concerning the shape and interrelations of a given society at a moment in time; and his *diachronic materialism*, concerning the dynamics of social change.[4]

In Chapter 4 I discuss the special theory[5] of capitalism. Marx would not be the controversial figure he is if he had not bequeathed a theory for his own epoch. I suggest that Marx's notion of the class composition of capitalist society is crucial here, and that when it is understood in the appropriately structural and abstract way it is proof against the conventional wisdom that it is outmoded by the growth of the middle class and the gradual disappearance of the traditional industrial proletariat. Some parts of the Marxist vocabulary have received immensely helpful clarification in the hands of analytical Marxists. I believe that work remains to be done in the case of class, and my arguments here are intended as a contribution. Sympathetic elaboration of Marx's basic claims, a consideration of their status and the sorts of considerations which would lead to their support or rejection, are missing because theorists have too readily assumed that his thesis about the polarization of classes in capitalism is so obviously wrong.

As my epigraph indicates, Marx's concern was to change the world. Chapter 5 deals with his proposals to that end. My reading makes Marx at once more and less extreme than received interpretations suggest. He is more extreme in his criticism of *all* forms of society based on commodities and markets, whether free-enterprise or state-controlled, and therefore more extreme in his outline of the future society. But his commitment to the working class as itself the agency of change, and the implications which follow from this for the importance of consciousness-raising and democratic organization, lead to a less extreme politics than would normally be attributed to him. The political philosophy I ascribe to Marx would be widely regarded as utopian. My own view is that this charge often springs from widely held but poorly supported theories about human nature, or from less reputable left-wing shibboleths, but I shall not argue that wider issue here.

To describe Marx as both a theorist and an activist fails to bring out how entirely merged these two properties are. It would be more accurate to describe him as a theory-impregnated activist or an activity-impregnated theorist. His attempts to change the world are not capricious or arbitrary but based on a heavily theorized view of it. Equally, even when he deals with the most abstruse theoretical question, what drives him is his commitment to fundamental social change.

These considerations will influence our assessment of Marx's success. His more ambitious claims may turn out to be false. This will not necessarily reflect on his case for social change, provided that sound reasons remain for the practical aim. For commitment to that aim is not, for Marx, some gratuitous act. I shall express this point by saying that many of Marx's claims have to be understood as *normative* in nature. That term, however, has so many different meanings that I should make the way I intend it explicit. In my sense, a claim is normative just in case its role is to have motivational force, to give someone a reason for acting. Two points need to be made here. First, normative claims are not necessarily moral. A statement that something will serve your self-interest, for example, is normative, but not moral. Secondly, there is no implicit contrast here between normative and descriptive matters. This is worth mentioning since many philosophers and social theorists shy away from anything 'normative', believing that there is such a contrast and that only matters of fact can be given rational support based upon objective considerations. There is no reason why matters of fact should not *also* be normative, in my sense; indeed, I believe they frequently are. The same can be said of explanatory theories: to explain something can often be to give someone reasons for acting in one way rather than another.

Marx often attempts explanations, but I believe there has been an overemphasis on his explanatory, at the expense of his normative, aspirations. No doubt this reflects many commentators' concern with forms of explanation on their own account. No doubt, too, I have overemphasized other aspects of Marx's thought, particularly the idea of collective identification. It does seem to me important, however, to recognize both that there is a normative aspect to Marx's pronouncements, and that many different kinds of statement can provide motivational force. Explanation as such is retrospective and theoretical; Marx's aims as such are prospective and practical.

Notes

1. I therefore refer to Marx's works by the date of publication rather than of composition, except for letters.
2. For that claim, see Tully and Skinner (1988); and for its relevance to Marxism, Graham (1981).
3. Jon Elster, however, has done sterling service in compiling and collating relevant passages. See Elster (1985).
4. G. A. Cohen credits Erik Wright with a similar distinction between 'Marxist sociology' (concerning the relation between elements within a given social formation) and 'theory of history' (concerning development of forces across history) (Cohen, 1988: 176–7). Allen Wood also distinguishes between explaining the economic structure of a society at a given time and explaining

the changes which the structure undergoes in the course of history. He urges that 'the most important application of historical materialism for Marx ... lies not in the first but in the second sort of explanation, the explanation of changes between historical epochs' (Wood, 1981: 75–6). This is true, but *what* changes is a society whose elements Marx wishes us to see in a particular configuration.

5. The nomenclature of general and special theory is implicit in Engels (1883) and is used by Carling (1986: 31).

/ t w o /

Basic Ideas

In this chapter I consider the basic ideas underlying Marx's more complex theories. These ideas are not necessarily propositional in form; they do not necessarily add up to *theses*. Sometimes, it is a matter of calling attention to Marx's orientation, his way of focusing on particular considerations. Chief among these is the fact that we are material organisms, with a distinctive history of acting to produce the means for meeting our material needs. Marx's belief that we do so in classes leads to an emphasis on certain kinds of collective, and affects the patterns of explanation and reasoning he is prepared to endorse. His collectivism, however, is compatible with his explicit acknowledgement of the existence and importance of individual human beings. This acknowledgement furnishes the first indication that Marx himself may quickly part company with much Marxist tradition.

2.1 Basic Materialism

The term 'materialism' is likely to suggest the doctrine that nothing exists except matter. Marx did not hold that view. In his special theory, much turns on his analysis of the commodity, the basic form of wealth in capitalism (cf. 4.1). He asserts that the commodity possesses non-material properties which are vitally important for understanding its nature. If we consider it as an object of exchange, 'All its sensuous characteristics are extinguished'; it has only a 'phantom-like objectivity' (Marx, 1867a: 128). The explanation of this lies in its possessing *value*, which is a 'supra-natural property' (*ibid.*: 149).

9

> Not an atom of matter enters into the objectivity of commodities as values; in this it is the direct opposite of the coarsely sensuous objectivity of commodities as physical objects. (*ibid.*: 138)

The form of materialism with which Marx's name is most famously associated is *historical* materialism. He did not use that expression, but he does refer to the 'materialist basis' of his method (Marx, 1873: 100; cf. 1867a: 493n). His complex views on history will concern us in Chapter 3, but one observation is in order here. In unguarded moments, commentators sometimes speak as if Marx's historical materialism were just one thing. Thus, William Shaw holds that it is 'an empirical, scientific theory' and rejects the claim that it 'must be understood or evaluated only in terms of some supposed philosophical framework' (Shaw, 1978: 2). Richard Miller suggests that the relevant Marxist principles 'are not empirical laws at all' (Miller, 1984: 233). G. A. Cohen ascribes to Marx and Engels an extraordinary confidence 'that every unprejudiced person could just see that [historical materialism] was true' (Cohen, 1988: 130). In contrast, I want to stress that 'historical materialism' covers a welter of different thoughts and ideas, not all of which have the same status. Part of the difficulty in evaluating Marx's ideas lies in disentangling the various components.

Embedded in his Preface to *A Contribution to the Critique of Political Economy* (the '1859 Preface') there is a more general materialist conception of human life. This consists of what I shall call Marx's *basic materialism*. He asserts that legal relations and political forms cannot be understood on their own and originate 'in the material conditions of life' (Marx, 1859: 20). 'The mode of production of material life', he goes on, 'conditions the general process of social, political and intellectual life' (*ibid.*: 20–21).

What is material life, and why should it be thought to condition other forms of life? Marx is adverting to a cluster of uncontroversial features of human life whose significance may not be sufficiently appreciated. Whatever else we may be, we are at least physical organisms, with certain needs whose fulfilment is a precondition of any life at all. Marx says:

> life involves before everything else eating and drinking, a habitation, clothing and many other things. The first historical act is thus the production of the means to satisfy these needs, the production of material life itself. (Marx and Engels, 1932: 39)

Without action of this kind, there is no social, political or intellectual life to worry about. *How much* life there is of these other kinds depends on how long it takes to produce for material needs. Moreover, material needs cannot be satisfied once and for all. They must be met recurrently. The production of the means to their satisfaction is 'a fundamental condition of all history, which today, as thousands of years ago, must daily and hourly be fulfilled merely in order to sustain human life' (*ibid.*).

Any living organism has material needs which must be recurrently met in this way, but we have a history of *acting* to meet those needs, *producing the means* to satisfy them. We 'can be distinguished from animals by consciousness, by religion or anything else you like'. But people 'begin to distinguish themselves from animals as soon as they begin to *produce* their means of subsistence' (*ibid.*: 31; original emphasis). In *Capital* Marx is concerned with 'labour in a form in which it is an exclusively human characteristic' rather than with the 'first instinctive forms of labour which remain on the animal level' (Marx, 1867a: 283–4). The difference lies in the conscious, purposive character of human labour: 'what distinguishes the worst architect from the best of bees is that the architect builds the cell in his mind before he constructs it in wax' (*ibid.*: 284).

The distinction between human beings and other animals may not be absolute. Elster argues that other animals also produce their means of subsistence, that some do so with tools, and that in doing so they act purposively (Elster, 1985: 64–6). Even if Elster is right, however, it does not follow that Marx cannot make a distinction by reference to the ability to produce one's means of subsistence. He can still plausibly argue that there is a massive difference of degree. Animals may use tools, but we have no reason to suppose that they develop anything like the immensely sophisticated instruments which human beings have for producing their means of subsistence. Animals may modify their immediate environment in more impressive ways than we sometimes think, but they have not literally modified the whole surface of the globe in very complicated ways in the course of those pursuits, as human beings have done in the recent history of the species. Animals may interact with one another in producing their means of subsistence, but not in the very complex sets of relations in which human beings have done, nor with a complex history of changes in those relations. All of this makes it reasonable to hold that there is an important difference between human beings and other animals which stems from the ability, in its specifically human form, to act so as to produce one's own means of subsistence.

Marx claims that the production of material subsistence in these ways is not only *exclusively* human but *universally* human: an abiding feature of the human condition rather than a feature found only at some times and places. It is 'the everlasting nature-imposed condition of human existence, and it is therefore independent of every form of that existence, or rather it is common to all forms of society in which human beings live' (Marx, 1867a: 290). Nature imposes this condition because it is not a Garden of Eden where people could meet their material needs with no effort, simply appropriating what was already available. Instead, they have always had to labour. In consequence, the existence

> of every element of material wealth not provided in advance by nature, had always to be mediated through a specific productive activity appropriate to its purpose, a productive activity that assimilated particular natural materials to particular human requirements. (*ibid.*: 133)

Moreover, often during the history of the species many people have had to spend much of their time in activity related to producing the means of subsistence, rather than in activities to which such provision might be regarded as a means.[1] Nature has often been relatively inhospitable. That gives a further reason to call attention to this abiding aspect of human existence. It is sometimes suggested that Marx has an Aristotelian commitment to the idea of labour as the distinctive function of human beings, with an associated commitment that the good for them is to realize themselves through labour. It may then be asked why it should be appropriate to pick out just that feature of human beings and endow it with such significance in the first place (cf. Arnold, 1987: 287). Marx can fairly reply that the history of the species, rather than he, has endowed labour with significance in the sense under discussion here.

This emphasis on the importance of material life constitutes Marx's basic materialism. It yields one obvious sense in which legal relations and political forms originate in the material conditions of life: they could not exist without such material conditions. This basic materialism must now be defended against an obvious criticism.

It is sometimes objected either that Marx's view consists of no more than a truism, or that his more ambitious claims simply do not follow from the platitude from which he starts. In this spirit, Miller objects to those who 'dilute Marx's theory to a thin soup of truisms to the effect that technology influences change and people don't do much thinking if they cannot eat' (Miller, 1984: 171–2). Shaw objects that the arguments put forward by Marx and Engels in support of their materialist conception of history are 'frequently flimsy and perfunctory . . . that men must eat and have shelter before they can pursue politics and philosophy, hardly shows the explanatory primacy of that realm' (Shaw, 1978: 59).

In a more extended argument, G. A. Cohen criticizes Engels's speech at Marx's funeral. Engels said that Marx had discovered the law of development of human history:

> the simple fact, hitherto concealed by an overgrowth of ideology, that mankind must first of all eat, have shelter and clothing before it can pursue politics, science, art, religion, etc.; that therefore the production of the immediate material means of subsistence and consequently the degree of economic development attained by a given people or during a given epoch form the foundation upon which the state institutions, the legal conceptions, art . . . have been evolved, and in the light of which they must, therefore, be explained . . . (Engels, 1883: 167)

Cohen says that this faulty piece of reasoning represents what is 'widely regarded, in Marxist circles, as at once a sufficient explication and a compelling defence of the basic outlook of historical materialism' (Cohen, 1988: 124). It is faulty because it involves the fallacy of equivocation: from the fact that we must act to satisfy our needs it follows that material production is the foundation of other activities in the sense of being indispensable for them, but not in the sense of being explanatory of them (*ibid.*: 127).

Marx is held to commit the same error. In *Capital* he replies to a critic who suggested that material interests predominate in our own time but not in the Middle Ages or in Ancient Rome.

> Marx thinks it extremely telling to point out, in response, 'that the Middle Ages could not live on Catholicism, nor the ancient world on politics'. This shows that he fell into the error that trapped Engels. (*ibid.*: 130)

These criticisms seem to me unjustified. Before we get to explanatory primacy, I have tried to indicate that in his basic materialism Marx already allots several different kinds of primacy to material considerations: not only must we eat before we do anything else, but the needs which call forth material production are recurrent and universal, and this fact has major repercussions for the way many of us spend much of our lives.

It may be said that the primacy of the material in these several senses is still a truism. But although no one but an idiot is likely to dissent from it when it is stated in these terms, it is another matter to allow awareness of these facts consistently to inform one's thinking, rather than allowing them to slip from view – to treat, say, political or religious affairs in isolation from these momentous facts about how we must act so as to provide our subsistence, and in that way to cease to give the facts their due weight. Hence, Marx insists that 'in any interpretation of history one has first of all to observe this fundamental fact in all its significance and all its implications and to accord it its due importance' (Marx and Engels, 1932: 39). Hence, too, his comment: 'how absurd is the conception of history held hitherto, which neglects the real relationship and confines itself to high-sounding dramas of princes and states' (*ibid.*: 48). In a similar vein, history may be seen as a series of *takings*; but the conqueror must adapt in various ways to the nature of the wealth which is being appropriated and 'everywhere there is very soon an end to taking, and when there is nothing more to take, you have to set about producing' (*ibid.*: 90). There is a natural tendency to think that the facts of basic materialism cannot be worth stating unless they either express some striking and non-obvious truth or provide a justification for the more ambitious theory of history. That is not so, however: many would assent to the truisms about material life but still, for example, pursue historical studies in a way which *implicitly* denied its centrality and importance.

It would be an exaggeration to say that basic materialism has nothing to do with Marx's more ambitious theory of history, but it seems highly unlikely that Engels attempted a deductively valid argument in its support at Marx's funeral. Certainly the presence of terms like 'therefore' and 'consequently' signals an *argument*, but not all (in fact, very few) arguments containing such terms are deductive. (Cf. 'This room is a mess, so the kids have obviously been here.' 'Another term in office for this government will lead to the destruction of civilized values, therefore you ought not to vote for them again.') He is more plausibly interpreted as putting forward a hypothesis (with more certainty than is warranted) together with the considerations prompting it. We might express it thus:

We are material creatures whose material needs must be met recurrently throughout life; material production to that end is essential for all people, at all times and places, and the effort which goes into that is absolutely central in human existence; therefore, (it is not a bad bet that) the way in which material production is organized will have an influence in other areas of life and will (help to) explain those other areas.

Construed in this way, Engels's argument still needs support. It rests on suppressed premises we might think there was no reason to accept; it may involve a slide from the centrality of the *fact* of material production to a claim about the centrality of the *way* in which material production takes place; and it does not yet explain the asymmetry between material and other aspects of life which Marx postulates. But it is still distinct from the decisively flawed argument which Cohen ascribes to him.

Marx's comment is similar. He does not think it a telling point just to say that earlier civilizations could not live on politics or religion. That comment is immediately followed by the words: 'On the contrary, it is the manner in which they gained their livelihood which explains why in one case politics, in the other case Catholicism, played the chief part' (Marx, 1867a: 176n). That, too, is an underdefended claim, but mention of the basic business of having to produce the means of life serves to call attention to the considerations which provide the *prima facie* grounds for thinking that material production may have explanatory primacy.

Basic materialism connects importantly with human beings' interests. Certain things are in our interests owing to voluntarily chosen objectives, but others are in our interests *regardless* of our chosen objectives. For example, if I make an autonomous decision to become a professional footballer or devote my life to spreading the Gospel, then it becomes in my interests to pursue certain activities and achieve certain states. But, whether I have made these choices or not, my being the sort of creature I am already dictates that I have an interest in an uninterrupted supply of oxygen and an intermittent supply of non-polluted water.

Marx's materialism emphasizes interests arising in this second way. Human beings have material needs which must be met; and in order to meet them, they must enter into relations which are both indispensable and independent of their will (Marx, 1859: 20). Consider an analogous case which brings out the nature of this indispensability and independence. Is there anything which a rational agent must want just by virtue of being a rational agent? Bernard Williams claims that, given that there are things which we want to bring about, we have a general dispositional want for freedom from coercion (Williams, 1985: 56–7). It is a parallel point to say that a rational agent must want a secured material existence in various forms; for that is a precondition for pursuing any more particular projects they may have chosen. Generally speaking, staying alive, in reasonable shape, is a necessary condition of doing anything else of any significance. Interests arising from that need are therefore of special and fundamental importance, and independent of any particular intentions or beliefs we happen to have.

Williams himself would not accept the parallel. He argues that the only good we can derive as being uniquely necessary for pursuing anything is freedom. Money in particular, he objects, is more important in some societies than in others (*ibid.*: 80). Marx would be the first to agree that wealth specifically in the form of money is important only in specific historical conditions; but he would argue, correctly, that the wealth required for subsistence is universally necessary.

Basic materialism constitutes a particular way of looking at human beings, concentration on particular aspects of their existence. It is the starting point for a conception not just of history but of class, of politics, even of practical reason. It leads Marx, in his analysis of capitalism, to treat people as 'the personifications of economic categories' (Marx, 1867a: 92; cf. *ibid.*: 178–9). It is the starting point for the construction of a set of theories whose object is to aid a change in the world, theories which are more ambitious and therefore more exposed than basic materialism is. The connection with interests is especially important, and this aspect of Marx's materialism is crucial for understanding the significance of the more ambitious theories.

Basic materialism is also the starting point for Marx's disagreement with the Young Hegelians.

> Since the Young Hegelians consider . . . all the products of consciousness . . . as the real chains of men . . . it is evident that the Young Hegelians have to fight only against these illusions of the consciousness. (Marx and Engels, 1932:30)

Marx also wishes to fight against the illusions of the consciousness which surrounds him, so that is not the locus of his disagreement. He recognizes that an important precondition of changing the world is precisely to change the way we conceive it. But he is not concerned with *just* changing consciousness. Reality itself must be changed, and that must include – and pre-eminently for Marx – the material reality constituted by the mode of producing material life.

2.2 Individuals

Social ontology addresses the question of what entities the social world contains. As with many philosophical questions, in some sense 'the facts' are not in dispute. There are physically discontinuous entities of human shape acting in society. What is less clear is the *significance* of this obvious fact, and in particular whether these entities ought to be the primary, ultimate or only focus of attention. An extreme form of ontological individualism would hold that *only* individuals should be regarded as real. Marx does not embrace individualism in this extreme form because classes constitute an ineliminable part of his social ontology (see 2.3 and 2.4). But individuals *also* form a part of it.

This is most evident in general statements about the nature of history. 'The first premise of all human history is, of course, the existence of living human individuals' (Marx and Engels, 1932: 31). The 'social history of men is never anything but the history of their individual development' (Marx, 1846: 173). He explicitly distances himself from the view sometimes attributed to Hegel – that individuals are the passive expression of non-human forces achieving their aims through history.

> *History* does *nothing*; it 'possesses *no* immense wealth,' it 'wages *no* battles.' It is *man*, real, living man, that does all that, that possesses and fights; 'history' is not a person apart, using man as a means for *its own* particular aims; history is *nothing but* the activity of man pursuing his aims. (Marx and Engels, 1845: 125; original emphasis)[2]

Marx similarly resists the temptation to see later historical events as the planned outcome of earlier ones, separately from human plans.

> History is nothing but the succession of the separate generations, each of which exploits the materials . . . handed down to it by all preceding generations. . . . This can be speculatively distorted so that later history is made the goal of earlier history, e.g., the goal ascribed to the discovery

of America is to further the eruption of the French Revolution. (Marx and Engels, 1932: 59)

He says that the communists make use of conditions created by preceding generations 'without, however, imagining that it was the plan or the destiny of previous generations to give them material . . .' (Marx and Engels, 1932: 87).

In apparent contrast, Elster argues that Marx 'had a fairly consistent teleological attitude towards history' (Elster, 1985: 109; cf. *ibid.*: 107), characterized as a view 'in which the earlier stages are seen as tending irresistibly towards the latter and as being explained by their contribution to the latter' (*ibid.*: 114). Specifically, it was

> because Marx believed history to be directed towards a goal – the advent of communist society – that he felt justified in explaining, not only patterns of behaviour, but even individual events, in terms of their contribution to that end. (*ibid.*: 29)

It is possible to believe that history is moving in a certain way, as Marx did, without believing *either* that it is being directed to do so, if that implies a director distinct from human agency, *or* that one can explain earlier stages by reference to later ones. Indeed, Elster seems to depart from his own characterization of teleological reasoning when he comes to substantiate his claim. He cites two passages occurring in unpublished manuscripts which are meant to point towards such reasoning: one because it 'is a quite extraordinary homage to the capitalist as the unconscious agent of humanity and civilization'; the other because it 'contains a blatantly teleological statement to the effect that the interests of the species always assert themselves' (*ibid.*: 115). Even if the passages in question do contain this,[3] these statements raise respectively the possibility of unconscious agency and, perhaps, of unconscious collective agency. These two possibilities do, indeed, provide important sources of understanding history for Marx, but they do not show that he regarded the movement of history as involving any agency outside the human race itself.[4]

The commonplace that individual human beings exist can be invested with different kinds of significance. One might emphasize their status as separate centres of activity or consciousness, giving relatively little attention to their interrelations, or to the constraints imposed by the environment. Marx dismisses that as 'the "pure" individual in the sense of the ideologists' (Marx and Engels,

1932: 93). Where he stresses that human history is the result of human beings' thoughts and activities, he also stresses the constraints under which individuals think and act, their interrelations and, as we should expect from his basic materialism, their material embodiment and its consequences.

Individuals 'work under definite material limits, presuppositions and conditions independent of their will' (Marx and Engels, 1932: 37; cf. Marx, 1859: 20); they 'make their own history, but not of their own free will; not under circumstances they themselves have chosen but under the given and inherited circumstances with which they are directly confronted' (Marx, 1852b: 147).

Society, he informs us, is '[t]he product of men's reciprocal actions' (Marx, 1846: 172). It 'does not consist of individuals, but expresses the sum of interrelations, the relations within which these individuals stand' (Marx, 1939: 265). Individuals must produce so as to satisfy material needs, and they must do so in society with one another:

> since their *needs*, consequently their nature and the method of satisfying their needs, connected them with one another (relations between the sexes, exchange, division of labour), they *had* to enter into relations with one another. (Marx and Engels, 1932: 481; original emphasis)

> Production by an isolated individual outside society ... is as much of an absurdity as is the development of language without individuals living *together* and talking to each other. (Marx, 1939: 84; original emphasis)

The starting point for understanding that process is, in Marx's phrase, 'socially determined individual production' (*ibid.*: 83).

2.3 Classes

Nowhere does Marx give a systematic exposition of his conception of class. In *Capital*, vol. 3 (posthumously published) he asks 'What makes a class?' (Marx, 1894: 1025). He moots the possible answer that it depends on revenue and source of revenue: for example, belonging to the class of wage labourers or capitalists depends on whether wages or profit are one's source of income. He notes the possible objection that this criterion leads to an infinite fragmentation of a given class: landowners, say, might be held to belong to different classes depending on whether their revenue came from fields, forests or mines, and similarly for other classes. At that point the manuscript breaks off (*ibid.*: 1026).

We need not suppose that Marx thought this objection precluded source of revenue as the criterion for identifying classes, but it has to be specified at the right level of generality. What puts you into the class of workers is precisely that the source of your revenue is *wages*, not that you receive wages as a result of working in a field rather than a forest or a mine. Class membership, in other words, depends on very general structural properties shared with others and on the relation to individuals who do not share those properties; it does not depend on superficial, brute, observable features. The structural properties may themselves be intelligible only in the context of a theory employing relatively technical terms, and it may therefore be far from obvious what the class composition of a particular society is.

On this view, a class constitutes one kind of *group*, where groups are defined as collections of individuals sharing some significant social property (cf. Graham, 1986b: 24). Consonant with basic materialism, Marx focuses on properties arising from individuals' objective, material circumstances. This distinguishes his conception of class from conceptions which classify individuals together on the basis of cultural similarity, political allegiance, or state of consciousness.

I shall suggest later that this interpretation of Marx's conception of class enables us to make best sense of his general theory, his special theory and his practical exhortations. It might be held, however, that I misrepresent his position in making his conception depend solely on material circumstances. David McLellan has argued, for example, that Marx 'had a dynamic or subjective element in his definition of class: a class only existed when it was conscious of itself as such, and this always implied common hostility to another social group' (McLellan, 1971: 155). Ralph Miliband argues that 'for Marx, the working class is not truly a class unless it acquires the capacity to organize itself politically . . . without consciousness, the working class is a mere mass . . .' (Miliband, 1977: 23; cf. Wood, 1981: 93).

Some passages in Marx encourage, but do not justify, these claims. In *The Poverty of Philosophy* he says:

> Economic conditions had first transformed the mass of the people of the country into workers. The combination of capital has created for this mass a common situation, common interests. This mass *is thus already*

a class as against capital, but not yet for itself. In the struggle . . . this mass becomes united, and constitutes itself as a class for itself. (Marx, 1847: 166; emphasis added)

He refers to the need for 'the *proletariat* . . . to *organize itself as* a class' (Marx and Engels, 1848: 87; emphasis added), and later argues that against the collective power of the propertied classes '*the working class* cannot *act*, as a class, except by constituting itself into a political party' (Marx and Engels, 1871: 270; emphasis added).

The added emphasis stresses that Marx distinguishes between *being* a class, on the one hand, and *organizing as* and *acting as* a class, on the other. In all these cases, the class is recognized as existing prior to any question about the actions it undertakes. The 'subject of discourse', the class, is identified by reference to the material conditions of its individual members, and various substantive comments are made of the entity so identified (cf. Cohen 1978: 76 n1). Certainly Marx has views on classes coming to act cohesively and for themselves, but their doing so is not a necessary precondition for singling them out in the first place.[5]

The same point applies to class consciousness. In the *Eighteenth Brumaire*, Marx observes that the French peasant proprietors live in the same situation but 'do not enter into manifold relationships with each other' (Marx, 1852b: 238).[6] He goes on:

In so far as these small peasant proprietors are merely connected on a local basis, and the identity of their interests fails to produce a feeling of community, national links, or a political organization, they do not *form* a class. They are therefore incapable of asserting *their class interest* in their own name . . . (ibid.: 239; emphasis added)

Again, Marx makes a point about the importance of class consciousness and political organization, but explicitly recognizes the existence of a class independently of these. Immediately before this passage he says that Bonaparte 'represents a class, indeed he represents the most numerous class of French society, the *small peasant proprietors*' (ibid.: 238; original emphasis), and it is their class interest which isolated peasants are incapable of realizing. Here, then, as in the other texts, *being* a class precedes (and is therefore conceptually distinct from) possessing any particular consciousness or shared perceptions.

Moreover, even if concerted action *were* a precondition for the existence of a class, it would not follow, as it might seem to, that a shared consciousness was also a precondition. People may *unwittingly* act together (cf. 2.4). Groups of people carrying on a struggle without a proper appreciation – or with a distorted perception – of its nature is a very important possibility for Marx. Members of a class may literally not know what they are doing.

There are sound reasons for keeping considerations of political consciousness and action out of the definition of class. Marx constructs theories *connecting* class position with these phenomena (cf. 3.3). It would be a bogus kind of support for such theories to pack these considerations into the concept of class at the outset, and it would reduce to a tautology some of the important claims that Marx wishes to make. If the amalgam of material circumstances and other aspects of life does not manifest itself in quite the way Marx claims, then, on the more extended definition of class which includes appropriate consciousness and political allegiance, it would turn out that there simply were no classes. That conclusion would clearly be perverse, and would miss some of the point of Marx's commitment to the importance of class in the first place.

But what is that point? The idea of class plays several roles in Marx's arguments. It has, to be sure, an *explanatory* role: it is supposed to help us to understand why people think and do what they do. But it has at least two further roles. One is *diagnostic*: before explaining social phenomena, we must have an adequate description of significant social features. For Marx, any description of society which omitted mention of groups of individuals similarly placed with regard to their relation to the means of producing the necessities of life would be radically incomplete. Basic materialism ensures the pertinence of *this* feature for any proper appreciation of a human society. Hence Marx's antipathy to the procedure which starts from the apparently concrete phenomenon of population, without specifying the classes of which population is composed and the elements (for example, wage labour and capital) on which the classes themselves rest (Marx, 1939: 100).

The other additional role, intimately connected with this, is *normative*. Classes are one kind of group, a collection of individuals sharing some significant social property. Often, such a property will imply a correlative interest or set of interests on the part of its possessor. If one is, say, a parent, a ruler, a subject or a teacher, then one acquires certain interests in those capacities. Given the importance of one's material position for the rest of one's existence, it is even more obvious that the source of one's revenue, and the circumstances surrounding its acquisition, will necessarily give rise to certain interests. (*What* interests, it may be far more difficult to say.) In that way, class position will generate reasons for acting.

Sometimes a social description is associated with what I have elsewhere described as an *escape-interest* (Graham, 1986b: 26). Take, for instance, the description *registered unemployed person*. We could say that those to whom this description applies have a certain interest – an interest, say, in seeing the level of unemployment benefit maintained or enhanced. But circumstances may be such that they acquire a far more important interest in its *ceasing* to apply to them. They have an interest in becoming employed persons or, better still, *un*registered unemployed persons who have large fortunes and do not need to seek work. Escape-interests raise special problems when weighed against other, more straightforward, interests in the nexus of practical decision-making. We shall see that for Marx some class descriptions are associated with just such escape-interests.

2.4 Classes as Agents

Though agency is not definitive of classes for Marx, it is a crucial part of his basic conception of society that, as a matter of fact, classes do act, and that in one sense their agency cannot be reduced simply to the agency of individuals. This helps to explain why his social ontology contains more than just individuals.

For Marx, individuals are relatively powerless: 'the "power of the individual" very much depends on whether others combine their power with his' (Marx and Engels, 1932: 395). Struggles by individual workers to limit the length of the working day 'prove conclusively that the isolated worker ... succumbs without resistance once capitalist production has reached a certain stage of maturity' (Marx, 1867a: 412). To protect themselves 'the workers have to put their heads together and, *as a class*, compel the passing of a law' to limit the working day (*ibid.*: 416; emphasis added). The struggle in which they do so is 'a struggle between collective capital, i.e. the class of capitalists, and collective labour, i.e. the working class' (*ibid.*: 344).

These observations may seem merely to reinforce the points already made about Marx's basic ideas. Individuals must produce their means of subsistence, and do so in interrelation with one another; class descriptions, like any descriptions, are implicitly general and therefore distinguish characteristics shared by a number of individuals. It is likely that shared or common interests then arise which can best be pursued collectively, but there is nothing here to disturb a resolutely individualist social ontology.

What does raise that further possibility is a number of (admittedly obscure) passages where Marx suggests a change in the direction of dominance between individual and class, so that the class concept no longer arises in a secondary way, merely via some general characteristic shared by a number of individuals. Instead, the class concept comes to have primary application, and then applies derivatively to the appropriate individuals. Marx says:

> the class in its turn achieves an independent existence over against the individuals, so that the latter find their conditions of existence predestined, and hence have their position in life and their personal development assigned to them by their class, become subsumed under it. (Marx and Engels, 1932: 69)

He is perhaps making a similar point in a further (equally obscure) passage:

> . . . the communal relationship into which the individuals of a class entered, and which was determined by their common interests over against a third party, was always a community to which these individuals belonged only as average individuals, only insofar as they lived within the conditions of existence of their class – a relationship in which they participated not as individuals but as members of a class. (*ibid.*: 92)

The distinctness of the class from individuals, and its dominance over them, also seem to be affirmed in a passage where Marx points to a contrast between a class-divided society and a family or clan. In the former case, the social character of individuals' activity appears as

> something alien and objective, confronting the individuals, not as their relation to one another, but as their subordination to relations which subsist independently of them. (Marx, 1939: 157)

These remarks suggest a distinct form of collectivism, perhaps best explained on more neutral ground than that of class theory. Take more or less clearly defined collective entities, such as clubs, juries or university senates. It is relatively clear what the boundaries of their membership are, when they are engaged in deliberation, when they have reached a decision, and when and how they are carrying out their decisions. The collective's activities consist of a given number of designated individuals themselves deliberating and acting, yet a certain kind of irreducibility attaches to the collective. We can properly describe the contribution which individuals make to its activities only by explicit or implicit reference to the collective itself. For example, Jane Smith may hold and express certain views as to whether the prisoner is guilty. But this does not have the appropriate significance; it is not contributory to the deliberations of the collective entity the jury unless she does so *as a member of the jury.* Similarly, a collective entity, an electorate, returns a government to power, and does so through the activities of the individuals who compose it. But my actions of placing a cross on a piece of paper or pressing a button on a machine are contributory to that process only in so far as they constitute *casting a vote as an elector.* In other words, there is an ineliminable backward reference to the collective itself in the course of explaining its relation to the individuals which comprise its constituent parts.

Closely associated with this feature is a second. The descriptions most pertinent for understanding the actions of collectives are often different from those which apply to the actions of their constituent individuals. Thus, it is precisely the act of casting a vote which the individual *qua* individual (or even *qua* member of the collective) performs; it is not that of returning a government to power. Similarly, I cannot declare war on Bolivia or decide to close down a department at my university. Only a state or a senate, respectively, can perform actions of that order.

A third feature of such collectives is their survival through time as a given collective independently of the survival of the particular constituents that compose them. West Bromwich Albion Football Club has been in existence since the 1880s, unlike any of its current members. In that respect a collective is, formally speaking, more like a species or natural kind than a set of objects.

The term 'collective' might be used to refer to a number of individuals who share a common property or a common experience. For example, what I *suffer* in some contexts may be properly specified only by bringing out the fact that I suffer it as a member of a given group. (The humiliations to which someone was subjected as a member of an ethnic minority might be a case in point.) Equally, collective *ownership* is a phenomenon pertinent both to Marx's understanding of the world and to his aspiration to change it (cf. Brenner 1976 and 5.1 below). It will be clear, however, that my own use of the term 'collective' as a noun ties it to cases where a number of individuals *act* together in concert.

The examples of collectives so far have all been conventionally constructed entities rather than ones occurring in nature, as it were. However, there is no reason to confine the category of collectives to this kind alone. Consider an analogy with individual agents. The collectives mentioned so far are cognate with the case of a highly ratiocinative individual agent, who self-consciously and explicitly goes through a process of deliberation and decision before engaging in a temporally distinct consequential process of action. We all approximate to that case some of the time, and there may be good reasons for taking it as central for some purposes. But in so doing, we may lose sight of the diversity of individual human action. Not everything we do is so clear and orderly, nor is everything so transparent. On the darker side of human behaviour there are cases where we act without prior deliberation, or out of unconscious motives which may be more or less hidden from us, or in ways whose significance is lost on us. It may be a matter of hard-won discovery for us to find out not just why we act as we do but even what exactly it is that we are doing. In these diverse ways, individual action may be unconscious.

There is something analogous to this in the case of collectives. Individuals might contribute to some corporate action without being aware that they were doing so. They might be unaware that they constituted a collective at all. They might be aware of this, but unaware of some of the collective's acts to which they were contributors, or aware of them but unaware of their significance. (Think of how a clique might exemplify some of these pos-sibilities.) There might, in short, be *invisible collectives*. We may miss this possibility if we rely on the pre-existing vocabulary of conventionally constructed collectives in compiling our inventory.

Consider a further possibility. Imagine a number of people who share a common social condition. They stand in a particular kind of subordination to some other group in their society, and in consequence suffer a number of serious privations. They share not only a common condition but a common interest in ridding themselves of it – in my earlier terminology, an escape-interest (cf. 2.3). But suppose they realize none of this: it is not reflected in their thoughts or their vocabulary, and their descriptions of themselves and others emphasize differences rather than simil-arities. Suppose they engage in no corporate action of the kind which is definitive of collectives in my sense.

Suppose, however, that if these people did realize the facts about their common condition and the common interests they share, then their combined talents and powers would be sufficient for them corporately to change social relations, in a way in which it would not make sense to think of their doing as individuals, and in such a way that they would cease to share those characteristics originally ascribed to them. Then, although they do not constitute even an invisible collective, they do constitute a *potential collective*. They are a group who *could* act corporately in a significant way, though *ex hypothesi* they do not.[7] Potential collectives can be historically significant. Arguably, for example, the knowledge that slaves *could* act collectively itself affected the way their owners treated them: recognition of this possibility itself shaped social relations (cf. Elster 1986b: 152–3).

Even conventionally constructed collectives vary greatly in nature, size, complexity and social importance. (Clubs are one thing and multinationals are another.) Some collectives in the modern world have resources, powers of recall and sweeping powers of action of a quite different order from anything which individuals as such could achieve.[8] This alone would be sufficient for admitting collectives into one's social ontology.

It is specifically *classes* as collective agents that enter into Marx's ontology. The significance of what individual human beings do (and what is done to them) is often brought out, for Marx, only when it is viewed as what they do *as* members of a class; and sometimes they act corporately *as* classes in ways which would not be available to them as individuals. The importance of these possibilities will emerge in each of the next three chapters.

2.5 Collective Practical Identification

The recognition of the reality of collectives changes the social landscape. It is no longer populated solely by individuals standing in relation to one another. Collectives are important social agents in their own right, and must be taken into account in any adequate description of the social world. But the story we tell about collectives is not something simply to add to the story we already have about individuals, as if these were two distinct things. Description of individuals is complete, and an account of their actions adequately informative, only if it includes information about any collective they belong to and the contributions they make to its actions. Just as important truths about the social world are neglected if the collectives which it contains are not specified, so important truths about individuals are neglected if only they and their relations with other individuals are described, with no mention of their membership of different collectives. Part of who or what they are consists in such membership, which may vary from families and clubs to electorates and political movements.

Collectives will also figure in any *evaluation* of the social world, and in practical decisions about intervening in it. We may relate to collectives either *externally* or *internally*, depending on whether we are a constituent in the given collective. Consider external relations. The fact that I stand outside a collective does not remove all question of practical implications arising from my evaluation of it. I may regard its actions as in some way untoward, and this may dictate a range of actions in my relations with it: avoidance, or attempts to neutralize or suppress altogether the untoward actions, perhaps. Generally, I may stand in a relation of conflict with a collective in ways which provide me with particular reasons for acting. This is an important case for Marx. In his special theory he stresses workers' relation to the capitalist *class*, and focuses on what the class does rather than on the behaviour of individual capitalists (cf. 4.4).

The case where we relate internally to a collective is more complex for practical reasoning, and is particularly pertinent for understanding Marx's political philosophy. When I am a constituent in a collective I have the option of thinking and acting *as* a member of that collective, and of endorsing or refusing to endorse what it does. A question of *practical identification* arises. There is a massive difference between collective *identity*, where that refers simply to one's membership of a collective, and active *identification*. It may in some circumstances be obscure whether or not I do belong to a given collective, but when that question is settled the question of identity is settled too. Not so with practical identification: that kind of active endorsement of what a collective does does not depend on the simple question of membership. I may be a member of a collective with which I do not identify and whose actions I do not endorse.

When is practical identification with collectives rational? One unproblematic source for such identification is individual self-interest. For example, I may belong to a collective formed by a number of individuals for the pursuit of a shared common interest, and the collective may have much greater power than I to realize that interest. Here, it may be entirely sensible for me to 'think outside myself', focusing on the collective enterprise and regarding its decisions as I would my own. Active identification is here mediated by individual considerations, but still may lead to different attitudes and actions from those which would prevail if I thought of myself *only* as an individual rather than as a constituent in a collective. It may be rational to identify with and act through that collective, even where its judgement differs from mine.

Reasons for identification can also arise more directly from the collective itself. I may believe that a collective to which I belong is engaged in promoting some end which is intrinsically valuable – anything from the preservation of the national culture to the spread of love. Of course I must myself embrace or endorse the ends in question, but I do not regard them as valuable because I have chosen them; on the contrary, I choose them because I believe they have value independently. If the collective is pursuing those ends, it will be rational for me to identify with it. As a special case of this, I may regard the interests of the collective itself as intrinsically valuable. This may be a distinct matter from the interests of the individuals who compose the collective. The interests of, say, a church or a football club are distinct from the interests of the individuals who compose them at a given time. This is illustrated by the fact that the interests of such a club may be best served by getting rid of the individuals who compose it, even if this is not in their individual interests. Relatedly, I may have a commitment to some irreducibly shared objective which can be achieved only by a collective itself. Winning a team game is an example. Here, my practical thinking is in one sense necessarily collective, since the objective to which it is directed is itself necessarily collective (cf. Jordan, 1989).

In sufficiently propitious circumstances, facts about a collective can be as much a source of motivation for individuals as facts about their own individual situation. When I am contributing to the decisions and actions of a collective, I can identify with them as if they were my own, and be as little justified in resisting them as I should be in thwarting my own decisions and actions. (I may *in fact* thwart them, either out of caprice or because I can see something to be said against them. But in both contexts, if this is less than can be said in favour of them, such thwarting is irrational.)

The possibility of collective motivation modifies a conventional picture of practical reason, according to which individuals are motivated by self-interest, arising entirely from their own concerns, and morality, arising from the concerns of others, external to them. Collective practical identification constitutes a third kind of input. It is external in the sense of originating outside the individual's skin, but not in the sense of being an imposed form of motivation originating in the interests of some distinct entity. If part of what I am is a constituent in some collective, then the interests of that collective can touch me far more closely than that. To be moved by the interests of a collective of which one is part is distinct from being moved *either* by shared individual interests *or* by altruism. This distinctness is not recognized by commentators who assimilate the case of class solidarity to that of altruism (e.g. Elster, 1985: 397; Little, 1989: 183).

Collective identification, however, is not always rational. I may be trapped in a collective whose actions are inimical to my interests. It may, indeed, be positively malign in nature. Collectives have no automatic call on our sympathies and allegiances as, arguably, other human beings do, nor are they embodied creatures in the same way. Moreover, even where identification *is* rational, it will compete with motivations from other sources: social identities carrying no implication of participation in collective actions, and autonomously chosen projects. Further, I am likely to belong to a plurality of separate, overlapping or mutually hostile collectives. I may, for example, be a parent, an elector, a cyclist, taxpayer, trade unionist and professional, and participate in collective action associated with each of these. These considerations will have implications for my practical decisions and actions, and will not all point me in the same direction. There is plenty of scope for conflict both between collective entities and within one individual.

Marx recognizes the phenomenon of collective identification and associated interests. We know already from his basic materialism that human beings' material embodiment occupies a special place in the determination of their interests and rational motivation. The fulfilment of certain material requirements is a precondition of our doing anything else. Now although collectives are not embodied in the same way as individuals, any actual or potential collectives to which I belong *by virtue of my material circumstances* will have a special relevance to my interests. On Marx's view, there both can be and are collective agents whose nature and activity have momentous consequences for the material circumstances of individual human beings. Collectives will therefore be an especially appropriate vehicle for the pursuit of interests, whether those of a collective itself or those of individuals sharing some common condition (or, indeed, diverse conditions with a common origin). For Marx, both one's material position and the connection between this and one's membership of collectives are sources of basic, fundamental interests, and therefore of motivation.

He locates collective interest in the communal interest of a group of individuals interacting in material production. There, he suggests, the communal interest

> does not exist merely in the imagination, as the 'general interest', but first of all in reality, as the mutual interdependence of the individuals among whom the labour is divided. (Marx and Engels, 1932: 44)

He recognizes, too, 'real ties' such as 'flesh and blood, language, division of labour on a larger scale, and other interests – and especially . . . classes' (*ibid*: 45).

However, he alerts us to the possibility of individuals' identifying with collectives where it is not rational for them to do so. The introduction of the division of labour and private property 'implies the contradiction between the interest of the separate individual or the individual family and the communal interest' (*ibid*: 45). Interests and identifications become complicated as a result of this contradiction, and especially with the arrival of the *state*. There, the communal interest takes an 'illusory' form which is 'divorced from the real interests of individual and community' (*ibid.*), but the resulting 'illusory communal life' is based on the real ties mentioned earlier. Collectives such as the state are 'substitutes for the community'. A state is composed of classes, themselves collective entities standing in conflict, and constitutes 'not only a completely illusory community, but a new fetter as well' (*ibid.*: 91).

Individuals may actively identify with the collective which constitutes the state, and do so on the basis of characteristics which they really possess ('real ties'), and which provide them with interests. But these interests are partial and particular, they 'run counter to the communal and illusory communal interests' (*ibid*: 45–6). A tension therefore arises. These individuals did not set up the power of the state, do not control it, and do not have reasons to identify with it (as opposed to identifying with groups with whom they share characteristics such as language or class). In consequence, the state appears as something alien rather than as an expression of their own power. It involves 'estrangement' (*ibid.*: 46) – a term employed in Marx's early writings to describe one's relation to the state, productive forces of society and products of one's labour (e.g. Marx, 1932: 69–70; cf. 1939: 157–8). A closely related, more concrete, thought occurs in his special theory when he describes the worker in capitalism as treating 'the social character of his work, its combination with the work of others for a common goal, as a power that is alien to him' (Marx, 1894: 178–9).

By implication, we have here a conception – albeit nebulously formulated – of an overall community with which it *would* be rational to identify, as well as one(s) which involve(s) a perversion of that identification. We are invited to envisage 'the community of proletarians . . . who take their conditions of existence and those of all other members of society under their control' (Marx and Engels, 1932: 92). 'In the real community the individuals obtain their freedom in and through their association' (*ibid*: 91–2). Freedom and association are crucial preconditions of individuals' actualizing their 'species-being', an obscure concept prominent again in Marx's earlier writings (cf. Marx, 1932: 74–6). Once again, too, clearly related but more concrete thoughts are present in later writings. In *Capital*, vol. 1, Marx comments:

> When the worker co-operates in a planned way with others, he strips off the fetters of his individuality, and develops the capabilities of his species. (Marx, 1867a: 447)

Misgivings might be felt over the introduction of the idea of 'transcendence of individualist motivation', especially in view of the historical link between Marx and Stalinism (cf. Cohen, 1990b: 43; Elster, 1985: 116–18). Does it not signify the absorption of individuals in a wider entity in an unacceptable way? Here it is important to remember that Marx's social ontology contains collectives *and* individuals. So far, he is simply confronted with a problem which confronts anyone who embraces an ontology sufficiently rich to do justice to the facts of our social life: how to integrate the interests of individuals with those of collectives of which they are part. Nothing so far would justify the conclusion that Stalinism emerges from this. On the contrary, Marx aspires after a unity which would preserve the importance of the individual:

> Only in community [with others has each] individual the means of cultivating his gifts in all directions; only in the community, therefore, is personal freedom possible. (Marx and Engels, 1932: 91)

'Free individuality' based on communal control of wealth is the way he expresses that aspiration elsewhere (Marx, 1939: 158).

2.6 Explanation and Rationality

Analytical or rational choice Marxists are centrally concerned with the explanatory adequacy of Marx's theories, and assess them on their own assumptions about explanation and rationality. Elster urges acceptance of methodological individualism:

> the doctrine that all social phenomena – their structure and their change – are in principle explicable in ways that only involve individuals – their properties, their goals, their beliefs and their actions. (Elster, 1985: 5; cf. Przeworski, 1985: 97)

Ontological and methodological questions are logically separate. It is possible to allow that there are irreducibly collective entities, but to insist that they should nevertheless not figure in explanation. Accordingly, it would be possible for Elster, whilst embracing methodological individualism, to recognize irreducible collectives, and for Marx, whilst recognizing collectives, to give them no role in explanations. It is not clear that Elster himself observes the distinction between ontology and methodology. He says, for example: 'According to the principles of *methodological* individualism, there do not *exist* collective desires or collective beliefs' (Elster, 1986a: 3; emphasis added). But collectives are genuinely absent from his arguments, separately from his methodological recommendations.

> A family may, after some discussion, decide on a way of spending its income, but the decision is not based on 'its' goals and 'its' beliefs, since there are no such things. (*ibid.*)

Similarly, although he postulates social as well as individual needs, these are social only in the sense of being socially caused, or being shared by several individuals rather than just one (cf. Elster, 1985: 70). They do not include needs which could be described only in irreducibly collective terms, such as the needs of a class, nation, race, or church.

Correspondingly, as Elster notes and deplores, Marx not only

postulates collective entities such as classes, but explains historical change by reference to their behaviour. Elster is sceptical about
the entry of collectives of this kind into explanation, and the
collectivist methodology implied (cf. Elster, 1985: 3–4). He allows
the explanatory legitimacy of Marx's comments on how the
Catholic Church consolidated its rule by recruitment. This, Elster
allows, was 'a corporate body, able to promote its interests by
deliberate action' (Elster, 1982: 458), but a body like the capitalist
class is not: 'capital has no eyes that see or hands that move'
(*ibid.*). Marx is guilty of postulating 'a purpose without a purposive
actor' (*ibid.*: 454).

Now I have already expressed doubts about how far Marx
discerns any purpose in history separate from the purposes of
human agents (cf. 2.2), but it is true that he is in no position to
postulate purposive actors in the present context. Although he
believes that classes have indeed acted as collective agents in an
important way in human history, he believes that they have
frequently done so under ideological illusions, not seeing or
intending their actions under accurate descriptions. However, this
does not preclude a commitment to *non*-purposive actors. Just as
an individual may act without a purpose, unwittingly or absent-
mindedly, so may a collective entity act without any awareness of
what it is doing or any intention to bring about a particular result.
The degree of co-ordination among its constituents may license the
conclusion that an invisible collective is at work. Nor need the
absence of purpose preclude an explanatory role for such facts.
Explanation does not always answer the question 'why?'. Pointing
to processes of this kind may explain *what* is occurring. The onus
on Marx, therefore, is to show that his account of past history is
plausible, even in the absence of individuals' awareness of
participation in collectives or identification with them.

In this respect Marx thinks the future must differ from the past.
We shall see in Chapter 5 that his overriding practical objective is
that members of the subordinate class in capitalism should self-
consciously act in unison to bring about changes which would be
unthinkable except as the act of a massive visible and purposive
collective agent. He has to provide members of that agency with
reasons for acting.

On the assumptions about rationality espoused by some rational
choice Marxists, this practical onus is as problematic as the
explanatory one. That an action is rational 'means that given the
beliefs of the agent, the action was the best way for him to realize
his plans or desires' (Elster, 1985: 9), though rational choice theory

'does not tell us what our aims ought to be' (Elster, 1986a: 1). Alternatively, rational action is 'action which is the best means to realizing (whatever may be) one's goals, given beliefs which are themselves justified by the evidence at one's disposal' (Elster, cited in Cohen, 1988: 56 n6).

On this conception, individual contribution to collective effort faces *the free-rider problem*. Suppose I desire some outcome which can be achieved only by the co-ordinated efforts of a number of people. Then I can argue that I usually have no reason for doing anything towards the outcome. Either others will bring it about, in which case my efforts are superfluous and I can still enjoy the benefits; or they will not, in which case my efforts are wasted and there are not even any benefits to enjoy. This will apply in all cases of 'public goods', whose enjoyment cannot be confined to those who took part in their production (except in the very rare cases where my contribution is crucial to whether the effort succeeds or not). Consequently, 'collective action is beset by the difficulty that it often pays to defect. The individual can reap a greater reward if he abstains from the action to get the benefits without the cost' (Elster, 1985: 347).

Many rational choice Marxists apply the free-rider problem to the case of class action (e.g. Buchanan, 1982: 89 ff; Cohen, 1988: 58–68; Elster, 1985: 347–66; Levine and Wright, 1980: 58; Przeworski, 1985: 96). Elster is not atypical in arguing that we must seek micro-foundations for such action.

> To explain the collective action simply in terms of the benefits for the group is to beg all sorts of questions, and in particular the question why collective action so often fails to take place even when it would greatly benefit the agents. (Elster, 1985: 359)

Accordingly, the 'motivation to engage in collective action involves, centrally, the structure of the gains and losses associated with it for the individual' (*ibid*.: 351). Class consciousness is 'the ability to overcome the free-rider problem in realizing class interests' (*ibid*.: 347).

Cohen addresses the doubt whether 'workers do have good reasons to fight for socialism, because of the free rider problem' (Cohen, 1988: 59). He rejects the solution that although I am surplus to requirements, I want to be among those who together achieve that objective (*ibid*.: 59–61). Instead, he argues that the reason 'which each revolutionary has to participate is that he can thereby reduce the burden on other revolutionaries in the task of achieving what they all seek', viz. socialism (*ibid.*: 63). The efforts of any individual worker are not necessary for the achievement of that goal, but it is still integral to what each individual seeks – namely, the lightening of others' burdens in that endeavour.

Rational choice Marxists approach these problems with a conception of rationality which denies them important conceptual resources for dealing with them. Three features of that conception are the implicit treatment of rationality as a property only of individuals; the assumption that ends themselves are outside the scope of rational criticism; and the confinement of rational action to an instrumental, means/end pattern. All three features can be questioned.

Seeing rationality as a property of individuals sits naturally with an exclusively individualist social ontology. But if there are irreducible collectives, then some questions of rationality are collective *ab initio*. Sometimes the question raised is not 'What is it rational for me to do?' but rather 'What is it rational for *us* to do?' Derivatively, an individual who has identified with a collective may raise questions of practical rationality in that form, rather than in an exclusively self-directed way.

The non-criticism of ends is part of a very widely accepted tradition: in effect the tradition which follows Hume in thinking that reason is and ought only to be the slave of the passions. Any tradition must begin from intuitions about what is and is not plausible, though emphatically (and especially for Marx, given his commitment to changing the world) it need not retain those intuitions. And there are competing intuitions which carry different implications for the possibility of rational criticism of ends. Suppose I act in ways which are appropriate for achieving my end, which is that of eating a housebrick. Since in almost all conceivable circumstances the end itself is insane, why should we regard such actions as rational?

Defenders of the Humean tradition might reply that if we regard the actions as irrational in these circumstances, we do so implicitly by reference to *other*, longer-term goals which I have. Hence, reason remains the slave of the passions, since desires or goals remain at the base of every rational motivation. However, agents' long-term aims may also be irrational: think, for example, of someone whose life is consumed by some entirely pointless obsession, such as never-ending washing or continually checking that a door is locked. If that is granted, the principle is established that rational motivation is not necessarily anchored even in long-term goals. Of course, it is a much larger project to devise a theory to justify this intuition, and it would be a contentious matter just where to draw the limits around clearly irrational long-term goals. But there are lines of approach to such a theory which are both plausible and congenial to Marx's own views.

We might begin from cases of basic physical sensation such as pain, and argue that it is self-evident that there are reasons for avoiding it, so that it is not possible to argue to the rationality of this kind of goal from anything more obvious (cf. Nagel 1986: 159–60, 171–2).[9] Material needs in general are one obvious source for rational goals, and a source which fits in well with the normative implications of Marx's basic materialism. If I need something, it is rational for me to embrace it as a goal and irrational not to, whatever my own desires happen to be. And some of my needs exist not relative to other, specific, goals which I may have, but only relative to *any* goals. Here, therefore, are considerations which can be mobilized in the interest of formulating a theory to back the intuition that goals can themselves be assessed as rational or irrational.

On the instrumental, means/end view, rationality is a property exhibited by individuals when their expenditure on any objective they choose is outweighed by the benefits accruing from such expenditure. So far I have argued that rationality is a property which can be extended to collectives and that objectives can themselves be rationally assessed. But it is further possible to question the central role given to the ideas of instrumentality, and expenditure and benefit. There can be rational actions which are not undertaken for any distinct, separate end, and rational actions where it is inapposite to seek some benefit to offset expenditure (whether an 'in-process' benefit, or a benefit residing in some distinct state of affairs). Going for a walk can exemplify both.

There is a large and indeterminate range of good reasons for acting, besides the favoured one of bringing about some result. One may act because of a wish to associate oneself with the efforts of some group or collective one has identified with; or as an act of self-expression; or in order to do what one regards as fitting, given one's nature, or what dignity demands, and so on. When Cohen asks rhetorically: 'Why should redundantly collaborating with other people make sense when no one would suppose that redundantly collaborating with natural agencies does so?' (Cohen, 1988: 61 n16), he is employing redundancy in the narrow, instrumental sense. If he were not, his question would not be rhetorical and there would be many answers to it, including those just mentioned.[10]

The need begins to emerge for a conception of rationality different from that of rational choice theory in all three respects mentioned above. It should leave a place for the criticism of ends and objectives; extend the notion of rationality beyond individual agents to collective ones; and allow that actions can be rational without conforming to the pattern of the economically achieved goal. Within the alternative conception, the phenomenon of practical collective identification can be justified as one source of reasons for acting.

It does not follow that the free-rider problem is thereby solved. Even on the alternative conception of rational motivation, it may still be possible to raise questions about the rationality of redundant contributions to collective action. (Going for a walk for its own sake, or joining in revolutionary activity as an expression of solidarity will preclude other actions and in that sense carry a cost which it may, overall, be irrational to bear.) A collective, too, might reason that unless its own contribution is crucial for the achievement of some end, it is acting irrationally in making it. (Imagine, say, a trade-union branch which argues that the strike will be successful even if it does not itself participate, so it would be irrational for it to do so.) But to address those questions with the alternative conception of rationality is to acknowledge the availability of much richer sources of motivation than are otherwise allowed. That is likely to change the way the questions are viewed and dealt with.

Elster remarks that collective action often fails to take place even when it would benefit the agents (Elster, 1985: 359). It is an open question whether this failure is more frequent than the *occurrence* of collective action which does *not* benefit agents, or than the absence of *individual* action which would benefit the individual. He makes large assumptions on the latter question. He argues that we should assume heuristically that individual behaviour is both self-interested and rational, and if not the former, then at least the latter (*ibid.*), though he claims that these assumptions are 'grounded in purely methodological considerations, not in any substantive assumptions about human nature' (*ibid.*: 6). Marx makes different assumptions, but they are not arbitrary or devoid of support. His belief that individuals act, both wittingly and unwittingly, as parts of collectives, and that when they do so wittingly this may be for good reasons or for bad, provides him with a distinct apparatus for dealing with these issues.

An account of human behaviour built on the alternative

conception of rationality remains in certain respects like rational choice theory. It does not remove from human behaviour the distinctive feature of decision-making. Elster argues that if the basic premisses of rational choice theory are denied, we are left with role theory, according to which individuals act as they do because they have been socialized to, and he objects to the idea of quasi-compulsive tendencies (Elster, 1982: 464). However, we should resist the suggestion of an exhaustive choice between rational choice theory and role theory, or the idea that the only alternative to rational choice theory is some theory of compulsion (cf. Hollis, 1987: 170). An enlarged ontology and a wider conception of rationality offer alternatives distinct from either of these.

However, there is a residual plausibility in rational choice theory in one respect. Where collective practical thinking is absent from individuals' minds, then even though they may *act* collectively, it is more likely that their own *intentions* will be individualist. This will then reduce the likelihood of their making rational practical collective identifications. A theory which ascribes individualist intentions to individuals is more likely to be correct in those circumstances. That is what Marx concedes when he describes the sphere of commodity exchange as 'the exclusive realm of Freedom, Equality, Property and Bentham . . . Bentham, because each looks only to his own advantage' (Marx, 1867a: 280). The point, for Marx, is to change that state of affairs. But that reveals the magnitude of the changes to which he is committed: they include massive changes in human consciousness.

Notes

1. Marx does not appear to give an unqualified welcome to circumstances where producing means of subsistence is less onerous. 'Where nature is too prodigal with her gifts', he suggests, she keeps the human being 'in hand, like a child in leading-strings' (Marx, 1867a: 649).

2. This quotation comes from Engels's contribution to the jointly authored *The Holy Family* (Marx and Engels, 1845). Ascription of a view to Marx on the basis of a work to which he was prepared to put his name seems to me at least as legitimate as quoting from material which he wrote but did not seek to publish.

3. The first says that surplus labour 'is truly labour for the benefit of society, even though, initially, the capitalist *collects* the proceeds of this surplus labour in the name of society'. The second says that the

interests of the species 'always assert themselves at the cost of the interest of individuals' (cited in Elster, 1985: 114–15; original emphasis).

4. Elster says that a teleological attitude is absent from *The German Ideology*, but present in texts both before and after it. He speculates on Engels's influence in the case of *The German Ideology* (Elster, 1985: 109–10). As I indicate, however, Marx's rejection of supra-human influences in history is evident in his early writings from the letter to Annenkov (Marx, 1846), and most famously in his later writings from *The Eighteenth Brumaire of Louis Bonaparte* (Marx, 1852b, republished by Marx in 1869).

5. Marx may appear to postulate concerted action as a prerequisite for a class's existing when he says of the emerging bourgeoisie: 'The separate individuals form a class only insofar as they have to carry on a common battle against another class' (Marx and Engels, 1932: 68–9). But here, similarly, a distinction can be drawn between a class's existing as a consequence of the conscious actions of individuals (being formed) and its existing regardless of their own acts and intentions. It is the *bourgeoisie* that Marx describes as splitting into various fractions before acting cohesively, and the bourgeoisie is a class.

6. I am not here concerned with the accuracy of Marx's comments about the French peasantry. Arguably, they were not isolated, and did enter into relations and engage in collective action. Cf. Taylor (1986: 6–7).

7. It might be argued that a potential collective as described *is* also an invisible collective: in failing to act in furtherance of their escape-interest, its members perform the collective action of unwittingly sustaining their collective oppression.

8. For amplification of this point and its implications specifically for the problem of world hunger, see O'Neill (1986).

9. It is consistent with this view to allow that the rational motivation arising from the avoidance of pain can be rationally overridden. The experiencing and also the infliction of pain can be rationally justified: but the point is precisely that they need to be.

10. It may seem that Cohen's solution to the free-rider problem, in the form he considers it, shares in my rejection of narrow instrumentalism. However, his own solution is supposed to ensure that a rational agent does 'make a significant difference to what happens' (Cohen, 1988: 61), since the goal is to lighten other socialist activists' burdens. On the broader conception of rationality which I sponsor, activity can be rational even if it does not have any *goal* in that sense at all. Accordingly, and paradoxical though it may seem, there can be good reasons for taking part in revolutionary activity besides that of individually making a crucial difference to the outcome. And that position Cohen does reject.

/three/

General Theory

In this chapter I discuss Marx's general theory of human society and human history. He might wish to disclaim adherence to any such theory, and some commentators argue that he does no more than project back into history the special features present in the case of capitalism (cf. Carling, 1986). Against his Russian critic Mikhailovsky he protests that he

> must metamorphose my historical sketch of the genesis of capitalism in Western Europe into a historico-philosophical theory of the general path every people is fated to tread, whatever the historical circumstances in which it finds itself . . . (Marx, 1877: 478)

However, Marx makes a number of statements, not apparently bounded temporally or geographically, which do sound remarkably like the historico-philosophical pronouncements he purports to reject. Ironically, the theorist who is most concerned to stress the particularity of historical circumstances seems to produce a theory which is ambitiously and ambiguously wide, transcends particular circumstances and applies indifferently to people at all times and in all places. It would in any case be impossible to study particular periods without a number of hypotheses about the phenomena under investigation, and Marx's own assumptions are strong and distinctive. I try to convey some of their richness and subtlety, and indicate how the different elements fit together. I begin by speaking unspecifically of 'the material' and 'the non-material', and gradually introduce further terms and distinctions in his vocabulary.

3.1 Synchronic Materialism

Marx's basic materialism invites us to concentrate on particular aspects of human existence. His synchronic materialism involves further claims about the primacy of these material aspects over other, non-material aspects. The sources for his views are a series of analogies and metaphors; a number of general non-metaphorical statements; and particular claims about particular societies which furnish illustrative material.

The most famous metaphor is the one of foundation and superstructure. People's production relations constitute 'the real foundation, on which arises a legal and political superstructure and to which correspond definite forms of social consciousness' (Marx, 1859: 20). Anatomical metaphors also occur. The *anatomy* of civil society (which Marx equates with the material conditions of life) has to be sought in political economy (*ibid*.). The form of production is 'organically related' to legal relations and the form of government (Marx, 1939: 88). Combining both metaphors, 'the material foundation' of society is 'the skeletal structure, as it were, of its organization' (*ibid*.: 110).

The content of the several metaphors signals the richness of the relations Marx postulates between material and non-material aspects of society. Material life is indispensable and, while not dictating the form of non-material life, it does limit the possibilities. Only a given range of possibilities is compatible with a given foundation or skeleton. The implication is that non-material institutions and practices will flourish, have marginal significance, or atrophy altogether, depending on how well they fit the material ones. For a society of commodity producers, Christianity 'is the most fitting form of religion', whereas the more limited relations of ancient modes of production 'are reflected in the ancient worship of nature, and in other elements of tribal religions' (Marx, 1867a: 172–3). A superstructure also obscures its foundation, and flesh serves both to protect and to disguise the skeleton which supports it. A 'science' may be needed to penetrate to what lies hidden beneath. Non-material aspects may hinder a proper appreciation of material life.

Metaphors do not constitute argument, nor do they constitute a sufficient explication of Marx's claims. In the 1859 Preface alone he claims different kinds of primacy for different aspects of material life. We are told that a *legal and political* superstructure *arises* on the economic structure. Then the mode of production of material life *conditions* the general process of *social, political and intellectual* life. Most broadly of all, we must distinguish between social change itself and the *'legal, political, religious, artistic or philosophic –* in short, *ideological* forms' in which people become conscious of it (*ibid.*: 21).

Marx sometimes expresses the primacy of the material in terms of reality (or truth). This follows another, crucial, analogy between the self-knowledge of individuals and of societies. We distinguish between 'what a man thinks and says of himself and what he really is and does' (Marx, 1852b: 174; cf. 1859: 21). So also with societies; and in historical struggles

> one must make a still sharper distinction between the phrases and fantasies of the parties and their real organization and real interests, between their conception of themselves and what they really are. (Marx, 1852b: 174).

Unlike 'German philosophy',

> we do not set out from what men say, imagine, conceive, nor from men as narrated, thought of, imagined, conceived, in order to arrive at men in the flesh. We set out from real, active men, and on the basis of their real life-process we demonstrate the development of the ideological reflexes and echoes of this belief-process. (Marx and Engels, 1932: 37)

Criticizing the kind of historian who ignores the 'real basis of history' Marx says:

> For instance, if an epoch imagines itself to be actuated by purely 'political' or 'religious' motives, although 'religion' and 'politics' are only forms of its true motives, the historian accepts this opinion. (Marx and Engels, 1932: 51)

Instead, he urges empirical observation to bring out the connection between the social and political structure and material production:

> The social structure and the State are continually evolving out of the life-process of definite individuals, but of individuals, not as they may appear in their own or other people's imagination, but as they *really* are; i.e., as they operate, produce materially, and hence as they work under definite material limits ... (Marx and Engels, 1932: 36–7; original emphasis)

These comments may encourage two different and unacceptable thoughts about the primacy in question. First, it may be thought that the contrast is between what people do (primary, true and real) and any kind of theory (secondary and illusory). This is obviously unacceptable, because there is no direct apprehension of what people do, separate from any theory about them. We can distinguish between what any society says it does and what it actually does, but we can take issue with what a society says about itself only by *ourselves* saying something different, and we are then left with the question of why our own view of the matter is to be preferred. There may be a convincing answer to that question, but clearly an acceptable theory must itself involve conceiving human beings in one way rather than another.

Marx recognizes this. His own method 'is not devoid of premises' (Marx and Engels, 1932: 38), and he acknowledges the difficulties which begin 'when we set about the observation and the arrangement – the real depiction – of our historical material' (*ibid.*). The removal of those difficulties is governed by premises 'which only the study of the actual life-process and the activity of the individuals of each epoch will make evident' (*ibid.*: 39). The results of that process can then be embodied in abstractions which arise from such study.

Secondly, it might be thought that the secondariness of non-material aspects of life consists in their being a mere residue or epiphenomenon, having no influence on anything to do with material life while aspects of material life do have an influence on them. There are passages in Marx which may seem to support this. He says, for example, 'The ruling ideas are *nothing more than the ideal expression* of the dominant material relationships . . .' (Marx and Engels, 1932: 60; emphasis added). This secondariness might be thought to be temporal:

> Reflection on the forms of human life, hence also scientific analysis of those forms, takes a course directly opposite to their real development. Reflection begins *post festum*, and therefore with the results of the process of development ready to hand. (Marx, 1867a: 168)

There are clearly echoes here of Hegel's remark that the Owl of Minerva spreads its wings with the coming of dusk, his idea that philosophy has an essentially retrospective role in comprehending events, rather than influencing their occurrence.

However, there are also places where Marx recognizes that non-material aspects of life, such as ideas, may not be wholly inert. One example, of some importance in his account of capitalism, concerns Aristotle's discussion of the value of commodities. For

Marx, the secret for understanding the issue lies in the equivalence of all kinds of human labour. But the secret 'could not be deciphered until the concept of human equality had already acquired the permanence of a fixed popular opinion' (Marx, 1867a: 152). This was absent from Aristotle's society, and prevented him from understanding a vital fact about material relations. Here, therefore, a fact about non-material life, the self-image which a society possesses, has an influence on the state of knowledge of material life.

Now it could be objected that this example shows only that theory is not necessarily inert so far as influence over *other theory* is concerned. It does not demonstrate any influence of popular opinion over anything which is actually done (or done in the course of material life). That is correct, but at other times Marx does recognize that possibility. In connection with the evolution of capitalist society, for example, he claims that 'Protestantism, by changing almost all the traditional holidays into working days, played an important part in the genesis of capital' (Marx, 1867a: 387 n92). Here, then, a religious form of life itself influences material relations. Moreover, it is reasonable to suppose that Marx believed his own theories had an important and non-redundant role to play in achieving certain practical results. The claim that no understanding of material forms of life is possible in advance of their existence is over-general and inimical to Marx's wider purposes. We shall see in 5.2 that it is a crucial feature of his proposed future society that its basic nature, at least, be understood in advance of its construction.

The primacy of the material, then, cannot be associated with an implausible distinction between untheorized reality on the one hand and universally suspect theory on the other; nor with the idea of the total inertness and passivity of the non-material. Nevertheless, Marx does think that a society's self-knowledge can go badly wrong. Its theory may be ideology, which gets things 'upside down' and is itself to be explained as originating in social relations (Marx and Engels, 1932: 37, 461). That will be precisely the form taken by theory which does not allow primacy to the material in the required ways (cf. Mills, 1985: 339–40).

In that regard, what Marx goes on to say about the Aristotle example is crucial and illuminating. Aristotle, we saw, could not provide a theory of value because the idea of human equality did not exist as a popular opinion in his society. But that idea itself

becomes possible only in a society where the commodity-form is the universal form of the product of labour, hence the dominant social relation is the relation between men as possessors of commodities. (Marx, 1867a: 152)

The presence, therefore, of an idea which has the potential for influence itself depends on material circumstances. The example in its entirety makes clear that Marx's synchronic materialism *both* embraces the mutuality of influence between the material and the non-material *and*, notwithstanding this, ascribes primacy to the material.

Hitherto, I have spoken of 'material life' or 'the material'. Marx makes further distinctions which raise a question about primacy *within* material life. Matters are complicated by his failure to employ a consistent terminology. In the 1859 Preface he says that it is the *mode of production* of material life which conditions the general life process (Marx, 1859: 20–21). Then, in a comment which reveals some of the anatomy of material life itself, we are told that people enter into definite *relations of production* which are appropriate to a given stage of their material *forces of production*. These relations are said to constitute the economic structure of society and to be the real foundation on which the superstructure arises.

In a simplifying move, I shall assume that the key terms are relations of production and forces of production.[1] 'Productive forces' is the more usual translation of the term *Produktivkräfte*, though 'productive powers' might be more appropriate, since it is less suggestive of wholly physical, non-human entities (cf. Wood 1981: 66–7). That, as we shall see, is to prejudice a substantive issue to some small degree by initial definition. Marx speaks here of relations of production in place of the wider terms 'intercourse' and 'commerce' (translations of the term *Verkehr*), used in very early works.

It followed from Marx's basic ideas that we should concentrate on the fact that human beings must expend energy in producing wealth to satisfy their material needs, and that they do so not as isolated individuals but in social relations with one another. The further thought now comes into focus that they must work *on* and *with* something.

This is one of the thoughts captured in the idea of productive forces. People inherit and work on a particular set of resources: raw materials, tools, and so on. But there are human as well as physical resources to call on: the skills, energies, productive techniques, which are equally a part of the legacy. Marx makes a similar distinction in his general discussion of the labour-process in *Capital*. That process in its general form, regardless of the particular social circumstances in which it takes place, consists of (1) purposeful activity, (2) the object on which work is performed, and (3) the instruments of that work. The second and third are designated means of production (Marx, 1867a: 284, 287).

Difficulties arise in the specification of productive forces and relations of production, however, when we take into account the implication, in some passages, of a primacy running from productive forces to relations of production.

In *The German Ideology*, Marx says that the *way* people produce their means of subsistence depends first on the nature of the means of subsistence they already find in existence, and that the form of their intercourse is 'determined by production' (Marx and Engels, 1932: 31–2). In a famous letter to Annenkov he says:

Assume a particular state of development in the productive forces of man and you will get a particular form of commerce and consumption. Assume particular stages of development in production, commerce and consumption and you will have a corresponding social constitution, a corresponding organization of the family, of orders or of classes . . . (Marx, 1846: 172)

In *Capital* we are told: 'It is not what is made but how, and by what instruments of labour, that distinguishes different economic epochs' (Marx, 1867a: 286), and:

Technology reveals the active relation of man to nature . . . and thereby it also lays bare the process of the production of the social relations of his life, and of the mental conceptions that flow from those relations. (Marx, 1867a: 493 n4)

In specifying *relations* of production, we might begin from the intuitive thought that they must include the ways in which people relate to each other in the course of producing the means of subsistence: subdivision of tasks, relations of domination and subordination, and so on. The primacy implicit here might then shadow that already described as holding between material and non-material aspects of life. Productive forces – a given set of technical and human resources – would limit and explain those relations. Relations would prevail which were most appropriate for the successful or efficient employment of given forces.

A problem, however, which affects *both* the specification of forces and relations *and* the question of primacy, is that in a number of places Marx explicitly includes 'modes of co-operation' in the category of productive forces. In *The German Ideology* he says:

> a certain mode of production, or industrial stage, is always combined with a certain mode of co-operation, or social stage, and this mode of co-operation is itself a 'productive force' (Marx and Engels, 1932: 41)

In *Capital* we are told, where many hands co-operate:

> Not only do we have here an increase in the productive power of the individual, by means of co-operation, but the creation of a new productive power . . . (Marx, 1867a: 443)

This affects the specification of the categories, because what we had taken to be characteristically relations of production now appear to be absorbed into productive forces. It also affects the question of primacy, because it is no longer clear that there are two separate categories between which a relation of primacy can hold.

One solution is to allow the category of productive forces to include such work relations and then define relations of production more narrowly, for instance as comprising relations of (or presupposing) *ownership*. The totality of these relations, the economic structure, would then be defined in terms of access to wealth, degrees of economic power over others, and the like. Forces and relations are kept separate, and there is room for a relation of primacy. A variation on this solution, given Marx's own unclarities, would place work relations in an intermediate category between productive forces and relations of production. Primacy can then be ascribed to the productive forces *vis-à-vis* the work relations, and a further primacy can be held to run *either* from the work relations to the relations of production *or* independently along one of two routes: direct from productive forces or direct from work relations. In other words, it might be that the efficient use of given productive forces required a certain set of work relations, and that those forces only mediately affected ownership relations because the work relations themselves favoured particular patterns of ownership; or it might be that both the given forces of production and the given work relations favoured those patterns.[2]

These possibilities impinge on another issue. Marx does not

always ascribe primacy to forces over relations in an unequivocal way. He speaks, for example, of the form of intercourse being 'determined by the existing productive forces ... *and in its turn determining these*' (Marx and Engels, 1932: 47–8; emphasis added). What people are, he suggests, 'coincides with their production, both with *what* they produce and with *how* they produce' (*ibid.*: 32; original emphasis). Further:

> The whole internal structure of the nation itself depends on the stage of development reached by its production *and its internal and external intercourse*. (Marx and Engels, 1932: 32; emphasis added)

People's 'material relations are the basis of all their relations' (Marx, 1846: 173).

These passages lead some commentators to conclude that relations sometimes have primacy. Marx, it is suggested, 'depicts both slavery and feudalism as structures maintained by the power of an economically dominant class ...' (Miller, 1984: 191–2). This particularly affects Marx's synchronic materialism:

> The most important features of a relatively stable society are largely explained by the needs and powers of what Marx calls 'the ruling class,' the group in the economic structure that, through its control of productive forces, mainly controls the surplus product ... (ibid.: 206).[3]

This interpretation, however, is *compatible* with ascribing primacy to productive forces within material life. It may be true that the relations of production are instrumental in lending stability to a given society, but also true that people at a given position in the relations of production can exert the influence they do because of the requirements of the level of productive forces (cf. Cohen, 1988: 15). Productive forces would then retain their primacy not merely within material life, but also (mediately) in their influence over non-material life too.

3.2 Explanation in Synchronic Materialism

Marx has now advanced beyond reminding us of the centrality of material life, in the ways described in his basic materialism, to espousing substantive theses about the connections between material and other aspects of life. Phenomena such as social, political and intellectual life cannot be understood on their own, and are conditioned by material life. However, there is a classical set of objections which challenge whether Marx can even state these theses coherently. These objections have been made by Acton and Plamenatz, and recently reinforced by Steven Lukes.

Acton argues that 'para-technological relationships' – laws or customs of property – are necessary if production is to occur at all (Acton 1962: 162). For example, if a hunting people turn to agriculture, then new rules concerning access to land become necessary. But, he suggests, 'productive relationships, in the sense of para-technological relationships, *are* moral, legal, and political' (*ibid*: 165; original emphasis). In that case Marx's primary factor, relations of production, '*comprise* moral, customary and legal [relations] and . . . therefore law and morals cannot properly be regarded as superstructures' (*ibid*.: 164; original emphasis). Thus, 'an analysis of the Marxist distinctions uncovers moral and legal and political relationships as aspects of the productive relationships themselves, and hence as aspects of the material basis of society' (*ibid*.: 165). In a theory asserting primacy among the elements which make up the purported base and superstructure:

> if the elements are never found apart, and if there are no means of separating them out statistically, there is no means of deciding whether the theory is true or false. The elements of the Materialist Conception of History are distinguishable neither in thought nor in fact. We have already shown that men using their instruments of production *are* men in social relations with one another. It is not a case of men using their productive instruments and of this *causing* social relations between them, as though there could *first* be something purely technological and *then* something social. (*ibid*.: 166–7; original emphasis)

Plamenatz objects that it is impossible to define relations of production except in terms of the claims people make on one another and recognize – 'in the broad sense of the word, laws' (Plamenatz, 1963: 281). It is then impossible to distinguish base from superstructure:

> . . . if law, in some narrower sense, is not involved in all kinds of social activity, morality and custom most certainly are. All properly social relations are moral and customary; they cannot be adequately defined unless we bring normative concepts into the definitions, unless we refer to rules of conduct which the persons who stand in those relations recognize and are required to conform to. (*ibid*.: 283–4)

Some of Marx's own comments encourage these challenges. In the 1859 Preface, he says that the phrase 'property relations' expresses the same thing in legal terms as the phrase 'relations of production' (Marx, 1859: 21). In *Capital*, he says that the exchange of commodities requires their owners to recognize each other as the owners of private property, which they do not take without consent:

> This juridical relation, whose form is the contract ... is a relation between two wills which mirrors the economic relation. The content of this juridical relation (or relation of two wills) is itself determined by the economic relation. (Marx, 1867a: 178)

Here a relation of primacy is asserted between the economic and the juridical relation, but it may be felt that this is a distinction without a difference. What is the difference between behaving in a certain way towards someone (e.g. not appropriating their commodity unless they consent) and recognizing them as an owner of that commodity? If there is none, then there is no difference between the economic and the juridical relation, and any claim of primacy collapses. The whole enterprise of distinguishing material from non-material life, and positing relations between them, fails.

However, Marx also indicates how this difficulty may be resolved. In discussing ownership of land, he says:

> Landed property presupposes that certain persons *enjoy the monopoly of disposing of* particular portions of the globe ... Nothing is settled with the *legal power* of these persons to use and misuse certain portions of the globe. The *use* of this power depends entirely on economic conditions ... (Marx, 1894: 752–3; emphasis added)

This suggests that terms like 'property' and 'ownership' can be used in a *de facto* or a *de jure* sense (cf. Cohen, 1970, 1978: 216–48, 1988: 30–36; Wood, 1981: 86). Something is my property in the *de facto* sense if I am able to dispose of it in accordance with my wishes, if I have *effective control* over it. Suppose, for example, I can ensure that I receive payment from a number of people for the use of a house. This may be owing to coercion, or their feeling an obligation to pay, or the existence of legal rules which confer rights on me and which they respect. So far as my *de facto* ownership is concerned, it is immaterial which of these factors is responsible for my effective control. On the other hand, it is the last possibility which indicates the *de jure* sense of property or ownership. I own something in this sense just in case legal or quasi-legal rules confer the appropriate rights upon me.

We can then distinguish between base and superstructure by reference to the *de facto/de jure* distinction. To have the power over some productive force, whether legitimately or not, is to stand in a basic relation of production to it; to have a right over it is to stand in a superstructural relation to it. The very fact that people sometimes have ineffective rights or illegitimate powers over such resources demonstrates the conceptual distinctness of base and superstructure (Cohen 1988: 34). This is compatible with powers and rights normally going together, and with the fact that the existence of rights is what ensures the existence of the corresponding powers – that 'in law-abiding society men have the powers they do because they have the rights they do' (Cohen, 1978: 232).

This last point serves to indicate that the Acton–Plamenatz objection has two distinct interpretations. On the first, the objection is that there is a logical or conceptual impossibility in making the kind of distinction Marx makes between, on the one hand, material life and, on the other, law, morality, and so on. The claim is that there is a similar logical or conceptual impossibility in the relations which he then affirms between these things. I have assumed this interpretation hitherto, encouraged by Acton's earlier remark that the different elements of the materialist conception of history are not distinguishable in thought. The objection, on this interpretation, does seem to be defeated along the lines indicated. Conceptual distinctions can be made which preserve the possibility of a primacy obtaining among those elements.

However, Lukes attempts to show that the objection on this first interpretation can succeed. He argues that what counts as an agent's *de facto* abilities will depend on what counts as a constraining or enabling factor. The answer to that 'is always relative to background assumptions and judgements, some of them normative' (Lukes, 1983: 112). Contract, for example, cannot be described in a norm-free way:

> The performance of contractual obligations is normally described in a vocabulary (paying wages, supplying services, buying and selling, honouring debts) which *already presupposes* the institution of contract and its regulating norms. (*ibid.*: 114–15; original emphasis)

If we avoid this vocabulary and stick to 'thin' *de facto* descriptions, in terms simply of handing over money, performing certain tasks, these will underdetermine the activities we wish to single out. Only some payments of money in some circumstances count as payment of wages, for example:

> ... how could the 'thin' non-normative description of transactions and dependencies between agents succeed in identifying *just those* transactions and dependencies which the normative relations involve unless the normative description were already, implicitly or explicitly, presupposed? (*ibid.*: 115; original emphasis)

Lukes does not mention the passage quoted earlier, where Marx speaks of the juridical relation in which owners recognize one another as such (Marx 1867a: 178), but that is an obvious case to cite in his support.

However, there is an echo here of the weakness in the original Acton–Plamenatz objection. Marx points to *aspects* of a complex, multifaceted social reality. He is not positing relations between discrete entities or processes. For that very reason we should not expect the kind of correspondence which Lukes demands between thin and thick descriptions, but rather just that underdetermination which he mentions, and an absence of logical entailments. A concrete act in the real world may be a case of handing over some money and *also* a case of paying wages, but not every case of the one is *necessarily* a case of the other. The matching would be too close, and of the wrong type, for Marx's purposes if it were. But where each description is *contingently* instantiated in one and the same concrete phenomenon, this allows some assertion of primacy and priority among its different aspects.

The question of whether we really have two aspects in the case of contract can be answered in this way. On the one hand, we have certain patterns of behaviour – no taking without prior consent, and so on. On the other, we have *recognition* of the other as an owner, precisely in the sense of acknowledging entitlement on that other's part (cf. the legal term *recognizance*). Here, too, we cannot infer the second from the first: I might refrain from taking without consent simply from fear of the consequences. But where the two do in fact coincide in concrete phenomena, it is then open to enter some hypothesis as to how they are related.[4]

On the second interpretation of the Acton–Plamenatz objection, the conceptual separability of base and superstructure is conceded, but their co-occurrence is taken as problematic. Relations of production cannot exist without laws, or morality, or customs – but then, since basic and superstructural elements occur together, we cannot establish any priority between them (beyond that already contained in Marx's basic materialism). This version echoes Acton's complaint that the elements of Marx's theory are not separable in fact: we cannot observe basic features which are then *followed* by superstructural ones.

Marx shares that starting point. He himself holds that material life calls forth various sets of attitudes, norms, legal and political arrangements, precisely because it has need of them and could not function adequately without them. As Cohen puts it, 'bases need superstructures' (Cohen, 1988: 34). But that may be thought to compound the difficulty, since it commits him to the idea that there is a two-way relation between base and superstructure. The problem then is how to reconcile 'the explanatory primacy of the economic structure over the superstructure and the latter's regulation of the former' (*ibid.*: 13). One of the most widely discussed issues in analytical Marxism has been Cohen's sponsorship of functional explanation as the means of reconciliation.[5]

It is important to be clear on the nature of the difficulties here. Sometimes temporal priority acts as a clue to the existence of causal priority. The temporal coexistence of relations of production and legal/political relations, as aspects of one and the same complex social reality, makes that unavailable here. However, causal relations do not exist only between temporally separate events. For example, two co-existent aspects of someone's character may be causally related, as when their obsessive will to establish superiority causes their disposition to behave aggressively in social interaction. The issue is therefore one of verification. Where there is no temporal priority, causal primacy has to be established in some other way.

Equally, where functional explanation is in question, it may be true that X occurred and is functional for Y yet false that X occurred *because* it was functional for Y. For example, Protestantism may be functional for capitalism, but it is one thing to establish this and another thing to establish that it explains the rise of Protestantism. As in the case of less complicated causal explanations, more is needed than merely noting the conjunction of two factors; and it is necessary to distinguish causal from accidental correlations.

Recall that synchronic materialism concerns the relations of a society frozen in snapshot, as it were. Some of these difficulties of verification may be eased by observing societies in motion, over time. Although relations of production cannot be observed without accompanying superstructural attributes, any pattern in successive relations of production and their accompaniments may allow inferences of subordination and domination to be drawn.

In 2.1 I expressed scepticism about viewing Marx's historical materialism as one set of claims with one status – say, that of an empirical hypothesis. It emerges from this discussion of synchronic materialism that there is, nevertheless, one strand here to which empirical evidence is centrally relevant. When relations of primacy and subordination, and the aspects of social life between which they are held to obtain, have all been clarified, it remains a matter for detailed investigation whether those relations obtain in a sufficient number of particular cases to justify the general claims. The appropriate means for establishing Marx's synchronic materialism therefore involves attention to a mass of empirical evidence about different societies. It differs in that respect from his basic materialism.

3.3   Class in Synchronic Materialism

Some of the richness and specificity of Marx's commitments is becoming apparent. The 'material considerations' of basic materialism (2.1) have been differentiated into forces and relations of production (3.1), and the primacy ascribed to them has become more complex (3.2). This refinement continues with the employment of Marx's basic idea of class in synchronic materialism. Its explanatory, diagnostic and normative roles (2.3) all reappear here, and primacy both within material life and between material and non-material aspects of life is re-expressed with the aid of the notion of class.

The 1859 Preface – a major source for understanding Marx's general theory – does not mention class explicitly. In contrast – at least in style and emphasis – are the opening words of the *Communist Manifesto*, part one: 'The history of all hitherto existing society is the history of class struggles' (Marx and Engels, 1848: 67).[6] Those struggles take different forms, depending on whether they take place between, say, freeman and slave or lord and serf. But through all these forms, 'the exploitation of one part of society by another' is 'common to all past ages' (*ibid.*: 86). It has consisted in the extraction of surplus labour from the subordinate class:

Wherever a part of society possesses the monopoly of the means of production, the worker, free or unfree, must add to the labour-time necessary for his own maintenance an extra quantity of labour-time in order to produce the means of subsistence of the owner of the means of production, whether this proprietor be an Athenian καλὸς καγαθός, an Etruscan theocrat, a *civis romanus*, a Norman baron, an American slave-owner, a Wallachian boyar, a modern landlord or a capitalist. (Marx, 1867a: 344–5)

In some places Marx suggests that we should identify economic formations of society according to the form in which surplus labour is extracted (*ibid.*: 325; 1894: 927).

It now becomes clear that for Marx class is defined not merely by relation to productive resources but also by relation to other human beings. This refinement makes it impossible to go on making unqualified observations about human beings in history, without recognizing that they are always class-located human beings whose conditions of life and life chances are very different one from another. The class relation, in its various historical forms, is antagonistic and curiously symbiotic: those who do not own the means of production are dependent on those who do for their livelihood, but by the same token those who do own the means of production depend on the efforts of their subordinates for sustaining their own more powerful and better-resourced position. The basic idea of the dependence of cultural and other forms of life on material life also gains refinement. Some may pursue these forms at the expense of others, who provide the material means for the leisure without which it would not be possible for the more privileged to do so (cf. Marx, 1867a: 667; 1894: 958; Marx and Engels, 1932: 475).

The refinement of the relation between material and non-material aspects in terms of class is exemplified in a thesis about intellectual phenomena:

> The ruling ideas are nothing more than the ideal expression of the dominant material relationships, the dominant material relationships grasped as ideas; hence of the relationships which make the one class the ruling one, therefore, the ideas of its dominance. (Marx and Engels, 1932: 60)

The class that rules in the material realm, therefore, also rules in the intellectual realm. Its conditions of existence 'are ideally expressed in law, morality, etc.', and 'are more or less consciously transformed by the ideologists of that class into something that in history exists independently' (*ibid.*: 461). This is done 'partly as an embellishment or realization of domination, partly as a moral means for this domination' (*ibid.*). But ideologists 'inevitably put the thing upside-down and regard their ideology both as the creative force and as the aim of all social relations, whereas it is only an expression and symptom of these relations' (*ibid.*).

The primacy of class is illustrated in Marx's comments about the Legitimists and Orleanists in *The Eighteenth Brumaire of Louis Bonaparte*. They constituted two fractions of the party of Order. In each case:

> A whole superstructure of different and specifically formed feelings, illusions, modes of thought and views of life arises on the basis of the different forms of property, of the social conditions of existence. The whole class creates and forms these out of its material foundations and the corresponding social relations. (Marx, 1852b: 173)

But 'illusions' is to be taken seriously here. 'The single individual, who derives these feelings, etc. through tradition and upbringing, may well imagine that they form the real determinants and the starting-point of his activity' (*ibid.*: 174). But it was 'not so-called principles which kept these fractions divided, but rather their material conditions of existence, two distinct sorts of property . . . the old rivalry between capital and landed property' (*ibid.*: 173).

Although Marx speaks of a whole superstructure of views of life arising on the basis of social conditions of existence, it does not follow that every aspect of given forms of thought is traceable to facts about class. It is significant that Marx concentrates here on political thought, that form of thought which is most germane to relations of power between human beings. (Thus, he illustrates the claim about the ruling ideas expressing dominant material relationships precisely by the example of political rule, almost as a pun.) He does claim that class relations reveal 'the innermost secret, the hidden basis of the entire social edifice, and hence also the political form' of class domination, but he allows that the same economic basis may display 'endless variations and gradations in its appearance, as the result of innumerable different empirical circumstances, natural conditions, racial relations, historical influences acting from outside, etc.' (Marx, 1894: 927).[7]

It is a familiar objection that Marx's claims about the centrality of class, as against other phenomena, cannot be sustained: that conflicts along religious, racial, national, linguistic or sexual lines, for example, have greater pre-eminence. Frank Parkin cites the way white South African workers and Protestant workers in Northern

Ireland identify politically and morally far more closely with their own bourgeoisie than with fellow workers in the subordinate ethnic group. He notes the awkwardness for Marxist theory 'whenever social groups act in blatant nonconformity with their assigned place in the formal scheme of things' (Parkin, 1979: 4). Marxism has to 'account for the awkward discrepancies between classes defined as embodiments of productive relations and classes as active political agencies' (*ibid*.: 25). Alan Carling stresses the importance of gender, ethnicity and age as 'dimensions of status . . . tending to seal the fate of individuals' (Carling, 1986: 57). Nove reminds us that 'Jewish capitalists went to the gas chambers together with their Jewish employees' (Nove, 1983: 19).

The general facts on which such objections are based are undeniable. The conflicts in which people become involved, the circumstances in which they live, the opportunities open to them, may all depend on some consideration besides their class position as defined by Marx. Can he accommodate these facts, consistently with the claimed centrality of class? I shall group together other loci of conflict and allegiance under the heading *cultural subordination*, and consider the general moves available to him. This inevitably involves oversimplification, since these loci are very different from one another, but it is important to see what responses can be made at the level of general principle.

First, cultural subordination may be straightforwardly material and class-based in form. For example, by virtue of my religion I may be consigned to the exploited class, providing the surplus labour for others to live on. The simplest case, which Marx can handle most easily, is where being a member of the subordinate religion is coextensive with being in the exploited class. He can argue that though the grounds of exploitation are religious, the nature of the exploitation itself is material in just the way he wishes to concentrate on. We can therefore continue to regard class as the fundamental feature in this case.

Carling objects that either not being in the subordinate religion is in itself sufficient for not being in an exploited class, or it is itself associated with property ownership, which then ensures that one is not in an exploited class. He concludes that being in the subordinate religion is 'the more fundamental feature of a person's situation either way, because in the first case the property variable has completely dropped out of the picture, and in the second it functions as an intermediate variable with no independent effect' (Carling, 1986: 59).

This objection is unconvincing. If the exploitation envisaged is strictly economic, then in one sense class has not dropped out of the picture at all. What happens to people economically is precisely what Marx directs our attention to, even if the reason why it happens to them (rather than someone else) is explained by their religion, or their religion and the further feature of property ownership connected with it.

A distinct case, perhaps occurring more often in reality, is where economic exploitation is not confined to the subordinate cultural group, but its *degree* is affected by cultural considerations. For example, suppose there are both Protestants and Catholics who are propertyless, but that Catholics fare worse on average *because* they are Catholics. Carling comments that here we have people for whom to be propertyless and to be Catholic are both necessary conditions of being in just that position, neither being sufficient on its own. Hence, he concludes, this is an instance of the 'irreducibility of the ethnic (likewise the gender) component in material exploitation' (*ibid.*).

This again seems to me relatively unproblematic for Marx. If we are concerned with strictly economic exploitation, then what puts one in the position of being exploited *at all* is one's lack of property. What determines the nature and degree of exploitation may well be factors to do with religion, gender or race. But that leaves a clear role for class as a basic consideration, just in the sense that it is, unlike being Catholic, a prerequisite of exploitation occurring at all. Marx's claim need not be interpreted as the claim that everything, not even everything about one's exploitation, is explained by one's class position.

In either of these cases, if Marx can establish the centrality of exploitation in the sense of its having a major impact on people's lives, then the influence of cultural considerations will not threaten his emphasis on class. Class position will generate important interests, and similarity of class position will generate important common interests, whether they are recognized by those who share them or not. For example, if being in the exploited class *at all* is a far worse misfortune than merely being in a worse position in that class than someone else in it, then a concentration on the lesser misfortune and a corresponding hostility and envy towards those who experience it will be a form of irrationality. It may, too, be a form of irrationality which merely serves to reinforce the existing class structure by promoting disunity among the subordinate class as a whole, whose collective powers might be immeasurably greater if they were united.[8]

Other cases are less easily dealt with: those, for example, of intrinsically cultural subordination, where the suffering of the disadvantaged is not economic, and therefore not necessarily class-based. Adherents of a given religion, say, are subject to social humiliations and prevented from worshipping according to its tenets; or women are subjected to demeaning and oppressive treatment. In the face of such non-material, intrinsically religious or sexual oppression, and of other cases where factors like language and nationality play a similar role, how can Marx continue to insist that class is central? Certainly the people involved in these relations may regard them as of more moment than their class relations. They may mind being a slave or serf or proletarian less than they mind not being able to worship their god, or being treated as inferior creatures.

Where intrinsically cultural subordination rather than extraction of surplus labour is in question, one's experience of it may still be affected by class position. It may be, for example, that only members of the exploited class suffer this subordination. In that case, Marx can argue that one's class position is indeed basic, in the sense of being instrumentally crucial for the occurrence of a form of subordination which the subject takes as basic, in the sense of being of greater moment in their scale of values. Even where the cultural subordination is suffered across the class divide, it may not be suffered in equal measure. For example, a female from the exploited class may suffer greater humiliations *qua* female than a female from the exploiting class. In that case class will play a role, albeit a diminishing and non-crucial one: it simply affects the degree of cultural subordination. Even that degree of salience of class disappears where cultural subordination is suffered in equal measure across the class divide (Nove's case of the gas chambers).

All Marx can argue here is that such circumstances are exceptional, that membership of the superordinate material class is, in general or very often, intimately connected with the possession of power sufficient to neutralize the threat or the degree of cultural subordination. He can argue that the class structure of a given society exercises a strong limiting function over other forms of subordination; that the appearance of the latter, the course they take, the ways of resolving them which are open to people, all depend heavily on their class relations. These are immensely complex claims, difficult to establish *or* to refute.

Consider a related argument about the connection of class to other phenomena. Przeworski argues that the Marxist tradition views class through the distinction between class-in-itself and class-for-itself, a distinction drawn from comments in *The Poverty of Philosophy* cited above (2.3). Class-in-itself occurs at the level of the base which 'is simultaneously objective and economic'; class-for-itself denotes 'class characterized by organization and consciousness of solidarity' (Przeworski, 1985: 51). The problem for this tradition is how the objective becomes transformed into the subjective, how a class at the economic level becomes a political and ideological agent. At the very least the tradition takes it that objective class position determines 'classes qua historical actors at the level of economic struggles' (*ibid.*: 71).

Przeworski's objection is that economic struggles are not determined uniquely by the system of production; they are affected by 'the totality of economic, political, and ideological relations' (*ibid.*: 67). Classes 'are not given uniquely by any objective positions because they constitute effects of struggles, and these struggles are not determined uniquely by the relations of production' (*ibid.*: 66). He therefore confronts the tradition with a dilemma. Either it retains the view that classes exist objectively at the level of relations of production – in which case that view will simply be irrelevant to the understanding of history at times when 'these classes do not develop solidarity and consciousness or when they have no political effects' (*ibid.*: 68); or classes are instead identified as organized political forces – in which case there is a serious problem in tracing these agencies back to places in the process of production. Seemingly, Przeworski's way out of the dilemma is to abandon classification altogether:

> The problem of the relation between objectively defined classes and classes qua historical actors will not be resolved by any classification . . . On paper one can put people in any boxes one wishes, but in political practice one encounters real people, with their interests and a consciousness of these interests. (*ibid.*: 65–6)

It is not clear how far these criticisms are meant to apply to Marx himself, as opposed to the Marxist tradition (and in particular Karl Kautsky). Przeworski acknowledges, for example, that Marx emphasized, especially in his historical analyses, the independent impact of ideological and political relations on class struggles (*ibid.*: 53) and instances the importance Marx attached to universal suffrage for the pursuit of class aims (*ibid.*: 70). However, since the conception of class he criticizes is in some respects strikingly similar to the one I have attributed to Marx, we should clarify how far Marx is subject to his strictures.

The 'class in-itself/for-itself' formulation is familiar, but it is not Marx's and it is too crude to capture his stance.[9] Elster observes that this formulation is so familiar that commentators tend to ignore the importance of another possibility, where classes exercise an influence not through their existence for themselves but through their existence for *others* (Elster, 1979: 101; cf. 1986b: 152). A group may not be consciously organized to pursue any goal, yet still impose constraints on decision-makers because of the way they perceive it. In that case, Elster argues that we should regard the members of that group as 'quasi-actors'.

This important possibility indicates phenomena standing between people's objective circumstances, on the one hand, and their fully and consciously articulated collective actions, on the other. (It is less clear that Elster would himself accept the further possibilities described in 2.4: of unconscious or invisible collective agents.) Groups of individuals might exhibit a degree of co-ordination, and even collectively achieve results, which they had not consciously planned to do. They might achieve exactly what they would have achieved *if* they had so planned. Their existence as collective agents might then be opaque both to themselves and to *anyone else* in their social environment. They might – to put it paradoxically – be a class for *no one*.

Intermediate points of this kind, between mere inert objective circumstances and fully conscious action, are crucial for understanding Marx's view of class struggles, for there is a corresponding ambiguity in the idea of class struggle itself. It may refer *either* to groups of people wittingly and deliberately engaged in hostile relations with each other, *or* to groups whose interests are opposed and who interact in certain ways which promote or thwart those interests *whether they are aware of any of this or not*. For Marx, class struggle is in progress in this second case, as much as the first.[10] He says: 'the social history of men is never anything but the history of their individual development, *whether they are conscious of it or not*' (Marx, 1846: 173; emphasis added). In describing class struggles through history he observes how oppressor and oppressed 'stood in constant opposition to one another, carried on an uninterrupted, *now hidden, now open* fight' (Marx and Engels, 1848: 68; emphasis added). In *Capital* he describes the 'protracted *and more or less concealed* civil war between the capitalist class and the working class' (Marx, 1867a: 412–13; emphasis added), and a recurrent theme is the way social processes go on 'behind the backs' of the social agents involved.

Erik Olin Wright observes how Marx's writings provide, on the one hand, 'abstract structural maps' of objective class positions and, on the other, detailed descriptions of the complex fragments of the collective agents actually involved in historical processes, which are often quite distinct from classes as objectively defined (Wright, 1985: 6 ff). Wright's own concern is with what he sees as Marx's failure to relate the two sets of maps. The question which I suggest arises from this disparate body of writings is whether there is any deeper truth beneath the literal falsehood of Marx's dictum that the history of all hitherto existing society is the history of class struggles. Marx recognizes that it is the history of much else besides. Are there, then, any reasons for putting those struggles at its centre? His answer relies on the richness of the original metaphors asserting the primacy of the material, as well as the multiple roles of his basic conception of class. His talk of class relations being basic, or central, or what is really going on, does not express one single idea.

Clearly, class in synchronic materialism is supposed to play an explanatory role. It is held in particular instances to influence and limit in various ways, though not necessarily to predetermine, other phenomena. Here, therefore, theses may be formulated in accordance with whatever explanatory paradigms are appropriate to Marx's synchronic materialism. The truth of such theses will be independent of people's self-perceptions in particular societies, and compatible with class struggles being affected by other factors than those specified in Marx's objective conception of class. Even if religious strife or sexual oppression is what we see or find ourselves caught in, class struggle may still have explanatory primacy.

Recall next that class has the diagnostic role of distinguishing a society's significant features. Exploitation as defined earlier is highly significant for those involved in it, whether they realize it or not. Even if they fail to develop solidarity and consciousness, or to form political movements, our appreciation of their condition increases understanding of the society of which they are a part. Where history is seen as anything more than the mere narration of a series of events, our understanding of it is enriched by an apprehension of who and what these individuals were and what they suffered.

Marx's determination not merely to understand but to change the world explains the further role for his conception of class in synchronic materialism: to give expression to people's interests. They may express certain preferences and engage in particular political practices, but their interests cannot simply be read off these facts. They can be mistaken as to where their interests lie: neither individuals nor societies necessarily know the truth about themselves. We have already seen the argument for the unique role of material considerations in this connection, as a prerequisite for pursuing most other – including non-material – projects (cf. 2.1). Involvement in either side of the exploitative relation carries implications for one's material security, and thereby for one's interests. Here too, therefore, Marx has good grounds for concentrating on it, regardless of whether the protagonists have such matters in their own consciousness.

Of course, we should not underestimate the difficulty of establishing the normative centrality of class. Even conceding the general point about the importance of material position, it is another matter to establish that one has any specific interests *qua* class member, and yet another to establish *what* such interests may be. Marx has to show both that practical identification with one's class is in one's fundamental interests, and that successful prosecution of those interests is achievable. Neither is easy.

The first is problematic precisely because individuals who are, say, peasants or workers are also, say, Catholics, dwellers in a particular village, or exercisers of particular trades and skills. All these roles also give rise to interests, and Marx must justify giving pre-eminence to those arising from class position as such. The second is problematic because it might be argued that classes are so large, and their members are scattered over such a wide geographical area, that people sharing those interests are incapable of acting in concert to realize them. If so, even an impeccable demonstration of the centrality of class interest will be of little use to Marx in achieving any practical result. In the light of this problem, it will be of great importance if he can demonstrate the existence of unconscious or invisible collectives, already acting in concert, whether in prosecution of their interests or not.

3.4 Diachronic Materialism

Time, and therefore history, are implicit in Marx's synchronic materialism: people stand in relations of production which are 'appropriate to *a given stage in the development* of their material forces' (Marx, 1859: 20). What is frozen in snapshot is therefore a temporal process. But his diachronic materialism explicitly addresses the question of change, and could therefore more justifiably be called a conception of history.

Productive forces gradually accumulate, aided by propitious relations of production, but given relations will not be propitious indefinitely for further development of productive forces. Eventually, they come to *fetter* those forces (*ibid.*: 21). At that point revolutionary change occurs; the relations of production are transformed, and then facilitate further development of the forces:

> ... in the place of an earlier form of intercourse [= relations of production], which has become a fetter, a new one is put, corresponding to the more developed productive forces ... a form which in its turn becomes a fetter and is then replaced by another. (Marx and Engels, 1932: 88)

Marx purports to discern a number of distinct epochs 'marking progress in the economic development of society': the Asiatic, ancient, feudal and modern bourgeois modes of production (Marx, 1859: 21).

Revolutionary periods initially consist in changes in the economic foundation, and eventually involve 'the transformation of the whole immense superstructure' (*ibid.*). But people's consciousness of change of this kind is to be explained from the conflict between forces and relations of production within material life.

> Thus, all collisions in history have their origin, according to our view, in the contradiction between the productive forces and the form of intercourse. (Marx and Engels, 1932: 90)

These collisions take on 'various subsidiary forms, such as all-embracing collisions, collisions of various classes, contradiction of consciousness, battle of ideas, etc., political conflict, etc.'. The subsidiary forms may erroneously be thought the basis of the revolutions, 'and this is all the more easy as the individuals who started the revolutions had illusions about their own activity' (*ibid.*: 91).

There are obviously strong parallels between synchronic and diachronic materialism. The primacy of material life and the threat of illusion are common to both. Many of the same problems of interpretation occur, and similar resources are available for dealing with them.[11] But the introduction of a historical dimension enables Marx to emphasize the *historical specificity* of different social arrangements. Needs and practices may be universal but nevertheless take different forms, depending on particular social circumstances. For example, only in some circumstances is the universal need for clothing met via the mediation of people whose special occupational role is to provide clothes for sale on a market: 'Men made clothes for thousands of years, under the compulsion of the need for clothing, without a single man ever becoming a tailor' (Marx, 1867a: 133). Similarly, only in some social forms do useful things appear in the guise of commodities, objects made specifically for exchange (*ibid.*: 153–4).

The stress on historical specificity blocks an erroneous pattern of inference. Suppose someone argues:

> The making of clothes is essential
> The making of clothes is tailoring
> Therefore, tailoring is essential.

Or again:

> People need clothes
> Clothes are commodities
> Therefore, people need commodities.

In each case, the first premiss is true without any time qualification, but not the second. Clothes are commodities, and making clothes takes the form of (professional) tailoring, only in certain societies. Hence it is invalid to infer from the truth that X is universally necessary to the falsehood that X *in this particular form* is similarly necessary. Marx's overriding interest in eradicating commodity society explains the importance of exposing and neutralizing this invalid inference. Otherwise, the defenders of commodity society seem able to argue for its retention on the strongest possible grounds: namely, universal facts about how human life must be. Marx starts from precisely that sort of premiss, but invests it with a sense of the variability of human societies and therefore emphasizes the transient nature of the society in which he lived.

Like basic materialism, the idea of historical specificity may seem remarkably exiguous. Surely, no one but a complete idiot would disagree that human society changes, in quite radical ways over sufficiently large timespans, and that in particular the features of material life look very different from one society to another? But it is another matter for this to be properly borne in mind in all theorizing about one's own society. No one would *argue* that the features of their own society were permanent, but that *assumption* might be implicit in their beliefs or actions.

Moreover, the theses of diachronic materialism are more specific, and therefore more vulnerable, than this. The idea of gradual accumulation of productive forces may be challenged, either because productive forces have frequently stagnated or regressed (cf. J. Cohen, 1982: 266), or because no one society exemplifies the development through epochs that Marx describes.

Neither of these difficulties seems fatal. Marx himself recognizes '[h]ow little highly developed productive forces are safe from complete destruction', instancing how the inventions of the Phoenicians were lost, as well as the manufacture of glass in the Middle Ages (Marx and Engels, 1932: 69). (Significantly, he adds that permanence is assured only when commerce is worldwide and based on large-scale industry.) In any case, even frequent loss of productive forces is compatible with an overall *tendency* to develop. Similarly, where distinct societies have some impact on one another, what has been called a 'torch relay' progression becomes possible, whereby developments which have occurred in one society need not be replicated in another, in which case we should not expect to see any one society exhibiting the patterns of every epoch (cf. Gellner, 1980).

More difficult questions of clarification and justification arise about the dynamic which is supposed to ensure this tendency to develop. Taken literally, Marx appears to hold that reaching the point of fettering is both a necessary and a sufficient condition for transforming relations of production. That it is necessary follows from a statement in the 1859 Preface:

> No social order is ever destroyed before all the productive forces for which it is sufficient have been developed, and new superior relations of production never replace older ones before the material conditions for their existence have matured within the framework of the old society. (Marx, 1859: 21; cf. 1850: 131)

That fettering is sufficient follows from his comment in the letter to Annenkov that people

> are *obliged*, from the moment when the form of their commerce [*Verkehr*] no longer corresponds to the productive forces acquired, to

change all their traditional social forms. (Marx, 1846: 173; emphasis added)

What does fettering amount to? We must make the best sense we can of a number of verbal formulations which stand in a degree of tension with one another.[12]

John McMurtry argues that Marx conflates the claim about fettering with a distinct and preferable one, according to which relations of production are revolutionized when either they or the productive forces stand under the threat of *absolute forfeiture* (McMurtry, 1978: 208). It is always the relations rather than the forces which are forfeited (*ibid.*: 206), where forfeiture of forces is defined as the permanent and qualitatively significant giving up of an achieved level of productivity (*ibid.*: 209 n11). McMurtry cites from two main texts to support this interpretation: *The Poverty of Philosophy* and the letter to Annenkov.

> As the main thing is not to be deprived of the fruits of civilization, of the acquired productive forces, the traditional forms in which they were produced must be smashed. (Marx, 1847: 117)

> On the contrary, in order that they may not be deprived of the results attained, and forfeit the fruits of civilization, they are obliged ... to change all their traditional forms. (Marx, 1846: 173)

He recognizes that to make the threat of retrogression in productive forces a precondition of transforming relations of production is to place a very stringent condition on the possibility of revolutionary change (cf. McMurtry, 1978: 213–18). It would follow that Marx was wrong in thinking that the time had come to get rid of capitalism, since there was no threat of permanent forfeiture of achieved levels of productivity. It is therefore an unattractive view to saddle him with.[13]

There is, moreover, a reading of these texts which ascribes a different view to Marx. In the first text, McMurtry assumes that the expression 'deprived of' governs the expression 'productive forces'. The unelliptical version of the first half would then read 'deprived of the fruits of civilization, *deprived of the acquired productive forces* ...' However, there is an alternative – and equally legitimate – interpretation, according to which Marx is referring to deprivation of the *fruits* of productive forces. The unelliptical version would then read 'deprived of the fruits of civilization, *deprived of the fruits* of the acquired productive forces ...'[14] We could take the second text in the same spirit, as hypothesizing the forfeiture of the fruits of productive powers rather than the forfeiture of those powers themselves. The results attained constitute an opportunity which may go unfulfilled if traditional social forms are not changed.

On this alternative interpretation, it is not the threat of forfeiture of productive forces which constitutes their fettering but rather their unavailability for *use*. A variant on this interpretation employs the idea of 'net fettering': used productive power, as a function of both the level of development and the degree of use (Cohen, 1988: 117). For example, one society might use its productive forces to a very high degree but have relatively undeveloped forces; another might use them to a lower degree but be massively superior to the first in the degree of their development. The second society might then achieve a higher net level of used productive power, though the first uses a greater *proportion* of its power.

The considerations outlined in Marx's basic materialism give ample reason why the use of productive forces is of acute interest to human beings. Their underutilization will provide at least a potential source of motivation for changing social arrangements, if they are the cause of this underutilization. Marx's call to abolish capitalism also ceases to be problematic on this interpretation, since part of his indictment of it rests on its failure to use productive forces: 'a great multitude of such forces could find no application at all within this system' (Marx and Engels, 1932: 76).

This interpretation is clearly incompatible, however, with the original fettering claim in the 1859 Preface, according to which the *development* of productive forces becomes fettered. As long as they are developing at some rate or another, relations of production will not be transformed; but they will be when such development stops altogether. That original claim suffers from a similar problem to McMurtry's interpretation. Marx saw capitalism as necessarily dynamic and expansive. 'The bourgeoisie cannot exist,' he said, 'without constantly revolutionizing the instruments of production . . .' (Marx and Engels, 1848: 70). But if so, then so long as *some* development of the instruments of production is occurring, at whatever rate, capitalism is not ripe for revolutionary change and calls to that end are premature.

On a modified version of that original claim, fettering consists not in the complete cessation of development but in its *relative* slowing down. Perhaps productive forces can continue to develop indefinitely within the relations characteristic of a given form of society, but there comes a point at which development within those relations is inferior relative to some other possible set of relations of production. That, it might be held, is the point at which relations become fetters and are transformed.

The modified version does not suffer from the same weakness as the original claim: it does not render it problematic why Marx should ever have called for a revolution against capitalist society even if its forces continue to develop. But it raises the related problem of whether anyone could be expected to listen to him. Why should the mere fact that some other possible set of productive arrangements would hasten development of the forces lead to such a fundamental transformation? Why should that abstract truth galvanize people in such a way?

It is not easy to find an interpretation of fettering which is plausibly attributed to Marx, plausible in its own right and consistent with his other commitments. It may be, of course, that such an interpretation is unavailable. But the difficulty may indicate that we cannot get clear on Marx's claim here, independently of seeing what reasons he has for making it. We have been introduced to a trajectory that history is supposed to follow, but we need to understand more about what fuels this trajectory. History, according to Marx, is made by individuals and classes in circumstances not of their choosing. Why might he think that people and circumstances combine to produce the pattern which he detects?

The reintroduction of the class dimension is especially pertinent. We know from the anatomy of synchronic materialism that the succeeding societies which develop productive forces are, on Marx's view, divided into exploiters and exploited, depending on the relation they stand in to those forces and to each other. Development of productive forces is not a project undertaken by the human race in concert and for its common benefit; it is undertaken in circumstances where the increased capacity is used to maintain privileged classes. These considerations are hardly likely to be irrelevant to the way in which societies progress.

3.5   Productive Forces in Diachronic Materialism

Already in synchronic materialism we have seen some of the complexity in the connections between forces and relations of production. Is there anything now in Marx's views which could plausibly explain the sequence: growth in productive power, aided by relations of production, punctuated by episodes of fettering from which new relations of production emerge, with continued growth in productive power? In this section I consider an influential interpretation put forward by G. A. Cohen: the *autonomous development thesis* (Cohen, 1988: 84).

The thesis is supported by general, non-social facts about human beings and their circumstances: that is, facts specifiable without any reference to social structure, in particular without any reference to social relations of production or class. In that vein Cohen argues that

> given their rationality, and their naturally inclement situation, people will not endlessly forgo the opportunity to expand productive power recurrently presented to them, and productive power will, consequently, tend . . . to expand. (*ibid.*: 86)

He regards it as important to establish this tendency independently – at least in part – of any *social* facts. If the reason for the tendency were *simply* that relations of production were inclined to propitiate it, this would clash with a further Marxian commitment: that the nature of the relations of production is itself to be explained by the level of development of the forces of production (*ibid.*: 84). An explanation of the tendency in social terms 'would deprive the tendency of its autonomy' (*ibid.*: 87).

It might be objected that this thesis is couched in terms of what 'people' do, as though it were not a significant consideration that history is made by people distributed into definite classes. Is this not precisely to forget Marx's admonition to take historical specificity into account? That may lie behind a problem raised by Levine and Wright. They describe as the *rational adaptive practices view* the view that people strive to develop forces of production in order that this will lighten their burden of toil (Levine and Wright, 1980: 54). They then object that in feudalism, for example, the impulse to develop productive forces did not come from people's material position considered in abstraction from their relations of production. What was rational from the position of a feudal lord would not have been so from that of a peasant (*ibid.*: 62–3). If that is correct, and development of productive forces depends on a description of people as identified by their place in the relations of production, then productive forces can no longer be regarded as undergoing *autonomous* development.

Now Cohen *agrees* with Levine and Wright in rejecting the rational adaptive practices view. He draws an analogy: a child has an autonomous tendency to grow up (it is not externally instilled, for example, by parents), but does not have any tendency to grow up autonomously (without assistance from parents and similar sources) (Cohen, 1988: 90). It is the same, he suggests, with the productive forces' tendency to develop. 'The tendency's explanation lies not within social relations, but in the sub-social facts about humanity' (ibid.: 90): in that way it is an autonomous tendency. But it is not a tendency to develop autonomously, and it may well require the assistance of propitious relations of production, which are 'the *immediate* source of development' (ibid.; original emphasis). Class is then left with a role to play, but a secondary one – secondary to 'a more basically grounded impulsion to productive progress' (ibid.: 91). But the postulation of this impulsion is held to be distinct from the rational adaptive practices view. The people who introduce new productive forces need not do so in order to lighten their own labour; rather, 'being rational, people retain and reject relations of production according as the latter do and do not allow productive improvement to occur' (ibid.).

But under what conception of rationality is it rational to act in this way? Even people convinced of the force of basic materialism might reasonably act to secure their own material needs without prompting general productive improvement. They might rob, or aspire to become exploiters. Why should rationality, via the medium of changes in relations of production, specifically point in the direction of productive improvement?

One reply might be that productive improvement necessarily implies improved provision, at least potentially, for human beings' material needs. That makes it a state of affairs which is just objectively desirable and therefore provides 'agent-neutral' reasons for being brought into existence (cf. Nagel, 1986: 159–60, 171–2). It is rational, rational for anyone, to bring it about. It is rational for people to support production-enhancing states of affairs, including changes in relations of production where appropriate, because *someone* gains from them, even if they themselves do not. This reply includes altruism, not just self-interest, within its conception of rationality, and is none the worse for that; but it ascribes such a recessive role to people's place in relations of production, and the influence this has on their perceptions, that it would be implausible as an interpretation of Marx's theory of history. It also credits them with an unrealistic degree of perspicacity, if rational considerations of this kind are supposed to have governed large-scale historical change.

There are two alternative replies, both fatal to the autonomous development thesis. First, it might be said that the exploiting class obviously gain from improved productivity, and they are in a position to *coerce* development-enhancing behaviour out of their subjects. In those circumstances, it is rational to do what you are coerced into doing because doing anything else is liable to be even less appealing.

This alternative is at best incomplete, since it fails to explain how one ruling class can ever be replaced by another – something of prime concern to Marx in explaining epochal succession. More importantly, in explaining the development of productive forces it makes ineliminable reference to relations of production. The rationality of development-enhancing behaviour is explained by reference to agents' position in a network of social relations and the consequences that follow. It therefore fails as an attempt to establish that there is any autonomous tendency towards development.

Secondly, it might be said that development-enhancing behaviour is rational relative to the beliefs of the agents, who are likely to think that they will benefit from general development even if they will not. This argument can claim textual support from Marx. In *The German Ideology* he argues that each ascendant class, struggling for domination, 'must first conquer for itself political power in order to represent its interest in turn as the general interest' (Marx and Engels, 1932: 45). It is likely to succeed in this representation. It 'appears from the very start, if only because it is opposed to a *class*, not as a class but as the representative of the whole of society; it appears as the whole mass of society confronting the one ruling class' (*ibid.*: 62; original emphasis). Moreover, initially this appearance is not even misleading. It

> can do this because, to start with, its interest really is more connected with the common interest of all other non-ruling classes, because under the pressure of hitherto existing conditions its interest has not yet been able to develop as the particular interest of a particular class. Its victory, therefore, benefits also many individuals of the other classes which are not winning a dominant position, but only insofar as it now puts these individuals in a position to raise themselves into the ruling class. (*ibid.*)

This reply gives more prominence to relations of production, and provides more resources for explaining epochal change. But it is even more damaging than the first reply for the autonomous development thesis. Development-enhancing behaviour is now explained via a notion of rationality which does not only depend crucially on considerations connected with relations of production; inasmuch as the interests of a new ruling class are not really universal, it also depends on considerations of ideological misperception. In short, class is no longer confined to the secondary role of facilitating a more basically grounded impulsion, described in non-social terms. The nature of that impulsion must itself be described in ways which give relations of production a crucial role.

There is, further, a problem of verification for the autonomous development thesis. How could we ever establish such a tendency if the productive forces must always develop with the aid of a particular configuration of relations of production? The analogy of the child's autonomous tendency to grow up is of limited help. It is unclear whether the maturation in question is physical or social, but either it is detectable independently of relation to parents and others, or it is not. If it is, the case is precisely *dis*analogous, since productive forces must always develop within some particular set of relations. If it is not, then the assertion of an autonomous tendency is just as problematic in the child's case as in our own.

This problem is emphasized by Cohen's distinction between *the reason underlying* the tendency for productive forces to develop and *the reason in a given instance* why such a development occurs (Cohen, 1988: 21–2). He insists that the underlying reason consists in the non-social facts originally outlined, but allows that the reason in a particular instance may be quite different. For example, the immediate reason why a capitalist introduces productively superior machinery may be to increase profits, but the underlying reason for productive progress is that 'capitalism prevails when it does because of the massive contribution it makes to the conquest of scarcity, however remote that end may be from the motivation of forces-improving capitalists' (*ibid.*: 22). A sceptic might ask if we need an underlying reason at all. Why should there be any more to this process than what we see: individuals and classes acting from motives which are distinct from anything contained in the underlying reason?

There is an answer. Separate explanations for why A occurred, why B occurred and why C occurred do not explain why the concatenation A+B+C occurred. Similarly, if there is a *pattern* of improvement in productive forces, that requires further explanation. Cohen relies on that fact, as he is entitled to, in introducing a sub-argument to supplement what he acknowledges are the 'remarkably exiguous' premises of his argument for the autonomous development thesis (Cohen, 1988: 87). The premise of this sub-argument is that societies do frequently improve their productive forces and rarely allow them to deteriorate. The conclusion is that the asocial premises express truths about circumstances which do have an impact on the world; otherwise we should not be able to explain the fact of frequent improvement and rare deterioration (*ibid.*: 99).

If it is true that productive forces frequently improve and rarely deteriorate,[15] that certainly requires explanation. But Cohen's argument is of the form 'What else could it be?' As he puts it, 'either accept that the asocial premises have great explanatory power, or offer an alternative explanation of the contrast between frequency of progress and infrequency of regress' (*ibid.*: 102). Perhaps the offer should be made.

3.6   Class in Diachronic Materialism

The question raised at the beginning of 3.5 remains. What plausible account can be given of human behaviour, on Marx's assumptions, which would explain the fact of succession and development of productive forces within a succession of different sets of relations of production? Like Hegel, Marx believes that there is a developmental pattern to history. Unlike Hegel, he postulates no intending agency which brings this result about. The problem, then, is to justify that view of history in terms of what human beings do, to sustain it in the absence of any appropriate agency which might intend to bring that result about (cf. J. Cohen, 1982: 254-6; Elster, 1985: 3-4).

An answer can now be elaborated without the constraints imposed by the autonomous development thesis, but with the aid of Marx's comments from *The German Ideology* quoted in 3.5. It can involve free use of considerations about the social relations holding between human agents and the consciousness with which they act. It can accommodate Marx's stress on the fact that we act as members of a particular class, rather than as human beings *simpliciter*. With these resources a plausible Marxian story is possible, which preserves a development thesis (but not an autonomous one) and explains discontinuities and their resolution.

As a minimum, suppose that people's rationality will lead them to have some concern with their material security and well-being, though less than a conscious and consistent appreciation of basic materialism would dictate. It will also be both class-specific and epoch-specific. It will take a different shape, say, in feudalism, depending on whether one is a lord or a serf. It will also be different, depending on whether one is a slave, a peasant or a proletarian. Not only will different locations within the same epoch generate different material concerns: so will locations of subordination which are separated by being in different epochs.

Why should this material concern have anything particularly to do with developing productive forces? I might be able to protect my material position by plunder, robbery, or some other way of free-riding on others' efforts. But, first, such parasitic or redistributive ways of securing one's material position are necessarily exceptional: they presuppose that material resources are available to take advantage of, that someone else is engaged in producing them. And, secondly, they reinforce the importance of class differentiation. For Marx, the extraction of a surplus from a subordinate class *is* a kind of plundering. This now suggests how there might be an impulse, in class societies, to develop the productive forces. If I am a member of a surplus-extracting class, the best way of securing my material position is to maximize the surplus extracted, and the best way of doing that is to compel hard work with efficient technology from the subordinate class. That is a highly class-specific reason for wanting to see productive forces developed. But we can call on the discussion in 3.5 to explain how a more general motivation of the same kind might be prompted: coercion or ideological illusion may induce a wish to see a similar development even in those who occupy the subordinate class positions in the given society.

Even if this is elaborated, the most it could explain is productive progress *within* a given society. It fails to account for large-scale transformation, epochal change. Indeed, the rejection of the autonomous development thesis makes that phenomenon in one way more mysterious. Explanation by reference to 'people's' motivations has been replaced by explanation by reference to class-specific motivations. But if the latter is sufficient to indicate why there should be development of productive forces in a class-divided society, by the same token it shows that the exploiting class has a vested interest in not seeing the relations of production change. What, then, could produce the impulse to move from one set of social relations of production to another?

To begin a reply to that, we need two additional, reasonable assumptions. First, a kind of minimal fettering thesis that not all new productive forces could be employed within absolutely any set of relations of production, that there is not infinite flexibility in this matter. (For example, modern industry could not function in a chattel slave society.) Secondly, that it will not always be evident in advance what the implications for relations of production will be from the development of a given set of productive forces. A dominant class would not wittingly see the development of productive forces whose employment would be incompatible with their continued domination – but they might well do so unwittingly, for it is a reasonable assumption that the social arrangements required for employing some new form of technology cannot be perfectly foreseen.

We can now see a dynamic which might lead from one form of society to another. The impulse to development within a society is liable to throw up possibilities which are not in the interest of the ruling class but are in the interest of some other group. This produces a new clash of interests, distinct from the clash characteristic of the settled class relations. The class which would benefit from the establishment of new relations of production may expect some support from other groups in any struggle against the dominant class, because these other groups are themselves in a disadvantaged position *vis-à-vis* the established ruling class. All the non-ruling groups will have a common enemy in the established ruling class, though for different reasons. 'My enemy's enemy is my friend' may or may not be a rational principle, but it is not difficult to suppose that it might act as a motivating force. In this way, a coalition may build up – of different groups with different real or perceived interests in social transformation.[16]

It may be objected that these suggestions cannot sustain claims about development of the order to which Marx is committed. They point only to possibilities, not to a pattern or tendency. There is, after all, no guarantee that the introduction of an interest in a technological innovation will result in a capacity to actualize that interest (cf. Levine and Wright, 1980: 59). There will be a ruling class with a strongly opposed interest and considerable reserves of power, and a prevailing ideology which, if Marx is right, will also sustain the already-existing relations.

In one sense the circumstances described – of technological innovation with potential benefits for a non-ruling sector – do not guarantee an appropriate change in social relations of production: there is no logical implication to carry us from one to the other. But that is not necessary for Marx's position. If causation is understood in terms of regularity and constant conjunction, rather than necessitation of some stronger and less easily explained kind, it remains an open question whether there are laws of development of the relevant type. It will look extremely implausible to assert any crude causal connection between (a) the appearance of new productive forces unusable without new social relations of production and (b) the introduction of such new relations. But then crude causal laws in general look implausible. A moderately sophisticated version of Marx's thesis is not ruled out, and has at least an initial plausibility.

The objection emphasizes, as does the interpretation distinct from the autonomous development thesis, the centrality of struggle. Accumulation of productive forces is not a smooth progression; it emerges not from the deliberations of rational individuals somehow detached from their class locations, but from a clash between interest groups where vital interests are at stake: a release of life for the exploiting class, who will not have to forfeit a proportion of their life in working to produce for their own needs; a loss of life for the exploited class, who will have to forfeit a greater proportion of their own life to provide for others' needs as well as their own. With so much at stake, it is little wonder that epochal transformation produces social convulsion.

That is what is at stake, whether those involved have a clear understanding of it or not. We know that on Marx's view they may have a very imperfect grasp of their own social relations, both at times of stability and during periods of convulsion. (The analogy with the imperfect nature of an individual's self-knowledge is drawn explicitly in connection with such periods of convulsion in the 1859 Preface.) There is ample scope here for the existence of invisible collective agents of the kind described in 2.4. Large numbers of agents may collaborate in the achievement of results of which they have no conception, or a flawed perception. If so, there will be correspondingly less likelihood of the kind of collective practical identification described in 2.5.[17]

One final point of clarification. If we interpret Marx as holding that there is a tendency for the productive forces to develop, which depends on matters arising from social relations of production rather than being autonomous, it does not follow, as Miller claims, that 'Marx's emphasis is not on the economic as opposed to the political' or that 'Marx does give political processes fundamental important [sic] when he writes history' (Miller, 1984: 227). So far as epochal transformation is concerned, Miller bases his argument on the claim that even at the outset fundamental episodes may be distinctively political in nature, as when feudal lords engage in wars with one another (ibid.). This argument fails to carry conviction because the agents engaged in these activities are themselves identified economically: to be a feudal lord is to occupy a particular economic, as well as political, role. There is no displacement, therefore, of the emphasis on material aspects of human life which, I have argued, underlies Marx's conception of society and of history. In that respect his basic ideas and his general theory are of a piece.

Notes

1. Miller (1984) argues that *mode of production* is the key term.
2. For permutations of these solutions, cf. Cohen (1978: 34–5, 112–13, 167; 1988: 5) and Wood (1981: 70).
3. A further complication is that, as part of his quarrel with 'positivism', Miller allows the definition of relations of production to differ from one society to another (cf. Miller, 1984: 198, 202).
4. What Marx can be defended from is the objection that it is conceptually impossible to keep base and superstructure separate. It is another question whether he does himself always specify basic phenomena in terms free of superstructural considerations. His specification of class relations in his special theory requires decisions of a kind which Lukes would probably call normative. Cf. 4.2.
5. I say relatively little about functional explanation here, partly because the ground has been so well covered and partly because it seems to me to give a slightly skewed impression of Marx's project to place questions of explanation at its core. For some of the major contributions to the debate about Marx and functional explanation, see Cohen (1978, 1980, 1982a, 1988), Elster (1980, 1982, 1985), Taylor (1986), Van Parijs (1981, 1982, 1984); and Wood (1986). Van Parijs (1984) attempts to do justice to the two-way relation between base and superstructure, and Shaw (1989) attempts to clarify Marx's remark that the ideas of the ruling class are in every epoch the ruling ideas (Marx and Engels, 1932: 60), both without invoking functional explanation.
6. While acknowledging that the language of class conflict may be absent from the Preface because Marx had to get it past the Prussian censor, Stanley Moore uses this contrast to argue that 'Marx's version of historical materialism is an unstable combination of two conflicting approaches to history – a dialectic of liberation and a sociology of change' (Moore, 1975: 213). He is critical of the former, which he associates with the pronouncements on class conflict, and suggests that Marx's attempt to understand social change in those terms rests on theories which 'are predictions of the future, rather than explanations of the past' (*ibid.*: 219). I believe that in his special theory Marx is less concerned with prediction than with providing reasons for action.
   Miller, on the other hand, expresses suspicion over paying close

attention to 'a preface to a book that [Marx] gladly allowed to go out of print, as superseded by later writings' (Miller, 1984: 175). But Marx is happy to quote both the preface and the book in his defence in those later writings (cf. Marx, 1867a: 175 n35, 169 n31). He similarly abandoned attempts to find a publisher for *The German Ideology*, and the explanation may be simply that special theory displaced general theory as his chief concern. If so, the 1859 Preface and *The German Ideology* remain prime sources for his general theory, and *Capital* becomes central for his special theory.

7. According to Elster, Marx thought 'objectively defined classes tend to acquire class consciousness, or else to disappear' (Elster, 1985: 391). It is difficult to find any passages which would support this generalization, though Marx has reasons for *advocating* class consciousness in his practical proposals (cf. 5.2). Elster further claims that Marx was 'right in the broader sense that the classes of modern society are all in possession of class consciousness, being well organized politically as well as economically' (*ibid.*). That depends on how Marx would identify the classes of modern society and what would count as *class consciousness*. See 4.2 and 5.2 respectively.

8. Elster criticizes this form of argument in Marx's hands, on the grounds that it is functionalist in form: 'From the fact that employers benefit from cultural division between workers, one cannot conclude that these divisions are to be explained by the benefits' (Elster, 1985: 393; cf. *ibid.*: 22: 'Ruling classes can exploit prejudices, but they cannot create them'.). But Marx's point may be neither functionalist nor explanatory. If divisiveness benefits the rulers, it is normatively pertinent to point this out in attempting to persuade the ruled to reject their rulers.

9. The contrast he draws is between a class *as against capital* and a class-for-itself (cf. 2.3, Marx, 1847: 166; Andrew, 1983: 580).

10. Elster implies that for a struggle to be a class struggle it must involve an attempt to abolish the class condition (Elster, 1986b: 152). But this is to conflate perennial class struggle with revolutionary class struggle. It is necessarily the former which is involved in synchronic materialism; the latter appears in diachronic materialism.

11. Not that one would necessarily give the same solutions in both contexts. One might ascribe certain kinds of primacy to *relations* of production in synchronic materialism and to productive *forces* in diachronic (cf. Miller, 1984: 206–7).

12. For similar discussions, to which I am indebted, see Cohen (1988: 109–23) and Elster (1985: 258–67).

13. McMurtry would argue to the contrary that the view is attractive, since it leaves intact Marx's prediction that a revolution to overthrow capitalism is inevitable. At this stage, the prediction remains unfalsified (but falsifiable) because the conditions in which to test it do not yet obtain (McMurtry, 1978: 211). I discuss the role of this

prediction in 5.3. Giving it up seems in any case preferable to supposing that Marx wasted so much of his theoretical and activist life trying to do something which his own theory precluded.

14. Curiously, McMurtry presents this quotation in a way which would considerably strengthen my claim by omitting the first comma, following 'civilization'. That renders almost obligatory the reading in which the threatened loss of the fruits of the forces is in question. The comma is there in the original text, however, so my favoured construction is only a legitimate one rather than the unavoidable one.

15. For Joshua Cohen's challenge on that question and G. A. Cohen's reply, see J. Cohen (1982) and Cohen (1988: 103–6).

16. Notice that these suggestions implicitly rely on the idea that it is the *use* of productive forces which becomes fettered. Exploited groups do not have to imagine productive developments which have not yet occurred; they merely have to imagine that developments which have already occurred are taken up.

17. These facts do not necessarily make the development thesis less rather than more plausible. People's consciousness during the convulsions may not accurately *reflect* what is going on, but it may still *aid* that process. For example, legitimation in one's own eyes may be so important that a group may be *more* galvanized by perceiving itself as acting to promote the good of humanity or for the greater glory of God than it would be if it perceived itself as merely promoting its own sectional interests.

/ f o u r /

Special Theory

M arx's approach to his own epoch is consistent with his basic ideas and his general theory. The study of non-material life recedes, and he concentrates on the features of material life specific to capitalism, in line with the normative and explanatory centrality of material life and the importance of historical specificity. People's relation to their own means of life and the consequences which follow from their separation from it must be understood, and may be obscured by our own thoughts. That is the central concern of *Capital*, the major source of Marx's special theory. Here, I do no more than convey and assess some of the main presuppositions of very complex views.

4.1 Capitalism: The Commodity Society

Capital begins with the distinguishing features of wealth in capitalism: 'The wealth of societies in which the capitalist mode of production prevails appears as an "immense collection of commodities" ' (Marx, 1867a: 125). Moreover, wealth takes this form in no other society:

> Had we gone further, and inquired under what circumstances all, or even the majority of products take the form of commodities, we should have found that this only happens on the basis of one particular mode of production, the capitalist one. (*ibid*.: 273)

> . . . a highly developed commodity exchange and the *form of the commodity* as the universally necessary social form of the product can

only emerge as the *consequence of the capitalist mode of production*. (Marx, 1933: 949; original emphasis)

... it is only on the basis of capitalist production, and hence of the *capitalist division of labour* within the workshop, that all produce necessarily assumes the form of the commodity ... (*ibid.*: 951; original emphasis)

The implication is that a society is capitalist if and only if its wealth *mainly* takes the form of commodities.

At earlier stages of production *a part* of what was produced took the form of commodities. Capital, however, necessarily produces its product as a *commodity*. (*ibid.*: 950; original emphasis)

What, then, is a commodity? According to Marx, it has two sides. It is or has a *use-value* – that is, it 'satisfies human needs of whatever kind' (*ibid.*: 125); and also an *exchange-value* – that is, it exchanges in certain proportions against other use-values. The distinguishing feature of a commodity, therefore, is that it is not merely useful but enters into *exchange*. More strictly, it is *produced for that purpose*, rather than merely happening to enter into exchange (*ibid.*: 166). Although exchange may occur peripherally and accidentally in many forms of society, according to Marx it predominates only in capitalism. Although there are other societies with markets, capitalism is the market society.

This suggestion of a biconditional link between capitalism and the predominance of commodities may seem puzzling. Surely, it may be said, capitalism is characterized by the existence of *capital* and of a particular class structure, rather than just the predominance of commodities? At different points in Marx's general theory we saw that societies might be characterized either by the nature of their productive forces or by the nature of their class relations. Is the second of these now not simply being ignored?

Marx believes that, in this case at least, he does not have to make that choice. Certain logical implications follow from the postulation of commodities. For example, being a commodity is a relational property, and a system of commodity exchange implies a division of labour. (If everyone provided for all their own needs, there would be no motivation for exchange.) But Marx goes well beyond such relatively uncontroversial implications. Implicit in the very idea of the commodity, he argues, are the central features of capitalism: the emergence of some commodity as money, the eventual use of money as capital, even the distinctive class relations of capitalism.

He argues that even a feeble development of commodity circulation brings money into existence (Marx, 1867a: 274). Suppose a state of affairs where commodities are exchanged, thus:

$$C_1 - C_2.$$

Then, before long, such exchanges will be mediated by money, thus:

$$C_1 - M - C_2.$$

Money has a multiple role: as a universal means of quantifying the ratios in which commodities are to exchange, as a medium through which to exchange them, as a standard of price, and other things besides (*ibid.*: 188–244). Marx argues that some pre-existing commodity takes on the monetary roles. Commodities do not exchange because there happens to be money; rather, there is money because commodities exchange (*ibid.*: 186, 211–12).

The very versatility and desirability of money ensure the motivation to engage in a new pattern of exchange, alongside these patterns of simple circulation of commodities, namely:

$$M_1 - C - M_2$$

in which money is exchanged in order to make more money. In this new pattern, money acquires a new and its most vital function: it becomes *capital* (*ibid.*: 248). The new pattern represents capital accumulation. However, Marx argues that very particular circumstances are required before money can acquire this role. Capital can emerge

only when the owner of the means of production and subsistence finds the free worker available, on the market, as the seller of his own labour-power. (Marx, 1867a: 274)

Capitalist production only really begins . . . when each individual capital [*sic*] simultaneously employs a comparatively large number of workers . . .

This is true both historically and conceptually. (*ibid.*: 439; cf. 1933: 1005)

The existence of a class which possesses nothing but its capacity to labour is a necessary prerequisite of capital. (Marx, 1849: 91)

But this condition is also a sufficient condition for the emergence of capital:

The production of commodities leads inexorably to capitalist production, once the worker has ceased to be a part of the conditions of production (as in slavery, serfdom) . . . In short, from the moment when labour-power in general becomes a commodity. (Marx, 1933: 951)

Once established, capitalism reinforces these relations. The existence of capital and wage labour are two sides of the same coin.

The capitalist process of production . . . reproduces the capital-relation itself; on the one hand the capitalist, on the other the wage labourer. (Marx, 1867a: 724; cf. 1933: 1005–6)

Thus capital presupposes wage labour; wage labour presupposes capital. They reciprocally condition the existence of each other; they reciprocally bring forth each other. (Marx, 1849: 92; original emphasis)

For Marx, therefore, the postulation of a commodity society is the postulation of much else besides. Many of his claims are strongly modalized. Where commodities predominate, their circulation *must* give rise to capital; capital *requires* wage labour; most generally, the exchange-value of commodities *must* come to dominate their use-value. No doubt this last claim is true in one sense: the idea of a commodity implies the hiatus of a market transaction prior to consumption, unlike, say, the case of subsistence production. But for Marx it is also true in a broader sense. The use of money as capital, to make more money, is bound to dominate its use merely to facilitate exchange of commodities. The accumulation of commodities as an end in itself becomes an inescapable characteristic of commodity society, and their use to meet human needs in any more direct way must become a lesser priority.

For some purposes, it is unnecessary to make such modal claims, but Marx bases his case for the wholesale abolition of capitalism on the nature of the character which capitalism is bound to possess. If he is wrong – if it is possible, for example, to arrange matters so that commodities do not predominate in the sense of demoting considerations of use and human need – then his drastic proposal would lose support. Instead of abolition, reform of capitalism could be urged, so as to remove the unwanted features. But for Marx to establish his case, commodity society need not be *conceptually* bound to assume a particular character: in that respect, he argues a stronger thesis than necessary. If it were true as a matter of *causal* fact that commodity society could function only with the priorities Marx claims, then his case would be reinstated as long as it were not defective in other respects. There would, of course, be familiar problems of verification in establishing such causal claims, but that is another matter.

The most vulnerable and most criticized of all Marx's claims about commodities are those embodied in his *labour theory of value*. He makes the *qualitative* claim that they all possess value, and the *quantitative* claim that their value is determined by labour. Value is distinct from, and explains, the exchange of commodities.

Commodities exchange in various ratios: x boot polish for y silk or for z gold, for example. Marx argues that these quantities 'express something equal' (Marx, 1867a: 127). An equation like

1 quarter of corn = x cwt of iron

'signifies that a common element of identical magnitude exists in two different things' and that both 'are therefore equal to a third thing, which in itself is neither the one nor the other' (*ibid*.: 127; cf. *ibid*.: 144–5). However, he holds that as use-values they have no characteristics necessarily in common. We must therefore abstract from their physical features and attend to them purely as exchange-values. Then, he suggests, we realize that being products of labour is the only property they have in common; and even then, not of any concrete form of labour (in which they may again all differ) but only of labour in the abstract. It is in virtue of this characteristic, therefore, that he concludes that a commodity is or has *value*.

Marx then stipulates that what determines any commodity's magnitude of value is the amount of labour-time socially necessary for its production, this labour-time being defined as 'the labour-time required to produce any use-value under the conditions of

production normal for a given society and with the average degree
of skill and intensity of labour prevalent in that society' (*ibid.*:
129). Any commodity's magnitude of value is then held to explain
– though, notoriously, not to be equivalent to – the price at which
it exchanges.

I shall not discuss here all the problems this theory faces.[1] The
qualitative claim has often been criticized on the grounds that
many items enter into exchange which are *not* products of labour:
gifts of nature such as land, wood, or water-power; and that in any
case commodities have other features in common, such as all
possessing some (not necessarily the same) use-value. The quantitative claim has been criticized on the grounds that goods may
exchange in a particular ratio because, say, they are very rare or
because someone wants them very badly, rather than because of
the amount of labour embodied in them.

Marx may have replies to some of these criticisms. He can argue
that by the time natural resources enter into exchange as
commodities, labour *has* been expended on them. Trading virgin
land, for example, presupposes some expenditure of energy on it: at
the very least, marking out its boundaries and perhaps protecting it
against encroachment. These resources are then like any other
commodity, in consisting of a substratum of matter on which
energy has been expended. It is less plausible to argue that labour is
the *only* property which commodities have in common. They will
differ in their particular use-values, but share the common
property of having *some* use-value or other, being wanted by
someone, and this might well enter into the explanation of their
value. Indeed, Marx himself seems to concede this. He says that
calculation of necessary labour-time itself depends on the level of
demand, that the labour-time which is *socially* necessary for a
given commodity depends on how much of it society wants (Marx,
1867a: 202).

These problems arise only if value is ascribed to commodities in
the first place, and Marx's *a priori* argument for ascribing value is
weak. True, commodities must exchange in determinate ratios,
and in that sense be brought into some kind of equivalence with
one another. We may, if we choose, represent this in the form of an
equation; but we should be cautious in what we infer. The
equation simply represents the fact that the owners of commodities exchange them in certain proportions. They presumably
have some reason for doing so, but it need not be the belief that
their commodities can be equated in any literal sense. The mere

fact of exchange does not imply the existence of some third item against which they are measured. Whatever may be the case with mathematical equations, therefore, it does not follow here that there must be some third unit in terms of which the equality of the two exchanged commodities can be expressed.

Indeed, the principle on which Marx relies here would prove too much. If two items appearing in an equation implied that both were equal to some third, distinct item, then by parity of reasoning they could be placed in an equation with that third item, from which it would follow that there was some fourth distinct item to which *those* items were equal, and so on *ad infinitum*.[2] That seems to multiply entities beyond necessity. This does not show that Marx's ascription of value to commodities is illegitimate. It does show, however, that the grounds offered for ascribing value are inconclusive.

A point of importance emerges for understanding Marx's rejection of capitalism, even on this most preliminary characterization. Consistently with his general theory, he identifies it not in political or legal[3] but in *material* terms. If it is *uniquely* identified by the presence of a vast accumulation of objects produced for the purpose of exchange, then the concept of capitalism as understood by Marx will range over a much wider collection of social forms than it does as understood by many other commentators. For example, for many the contrast between capitalism and socialism rests on the distinction between private and state ownership. For Marx the crucial question would be: private or state ownership of what? If it is commodities, as would be implied by the existence of a market as the predominant form of economic transaction, then some form of capitalist society will still be in existence. A sharp contrast between capitalism and socialism would then have to be made out in some other terms.

This issue is important not merely for the academic question of Marx interpretation. There is also the practical political question of how best to characterize those societies which, for much of the twentieth century, claimed Marx's imprimatur and distinguished themselves from other societies by use of the distinction between capitalism and socialism. If Western societies were happy to accept these characterizations, and vice versa, it can easily seem that there is no issue here. But terms like 'capitalist' and 'socialist' are not mere labels; they come with theoretical and political baggage attached to them, and my point in this section is to indicate some of the theoretical baggage in Marx's case. Bizarre and unusual though it may seem, it is not at all clear that the 'socialist' countries now opting for 'capitalist' economies were non-capitalist in Marx's sense.[4]

4.2 Class in Special Theory

Following the thesis of his general theory that the history of all hitherto existing society has been the history of class struggles, Marx characterizes class struggle in the capitalist era:

> Society as a whole is more and more splitting up into two great hostile camps, into two great classes directly facing each other: the bourgeoisie and proletariat. (Marx and Engels, 1848: 68)

His dominant view is that capitalism's relations of production consist in this polarization. It is true that he refers, for example, to 'the *three* great classes of modern society' in the famous last chapter of *Capital*, vol. 3, described at the beginning of 2.3 (Marx, 1894: 1025; emphasis added; cf. Marx, 1939: 108). It has also been argued that whereas in his abstract writings the polarization is posited, in his concrete writings on politics and history we are allowed a much more fragmented picture (Wright, 1985: 7). However, the three classes in question are wage labourers, capitalists and landowners, and Marx argues that the latter, third element, which is not distinctive of capitalism, tends to disappear into the polarization (Marx, 1894: 1025). Moreover, he reasserts the polarization thesis even in his political writings, as in *The Class Struggles in France*, where he describes the insurrection of 22 June 'in which the first great battle was fought between the two great classes which divide modern society' (Marx, 1850: 58).

Both before and after the *Communist Manifesto* Marx reasserts the polarization. In the *Economic and Philosophic Manuscripts* he refers to the abolition of the distinction between capitalist and landowner, 'so that there remain altogether only two classes of the population – the working class and the class of capitalists' (Marx, 1932: 61), and to the idea that 'finally the distinction between capitalist and land-rentier, like that between the tiller of the soil and the factory-worker, disappears and that the whole of society must fall apart into the two classes – the property-*owners* and the propertiless *workers*' (*ibid*.: 67; original emphasis). In *Capital* he mentions 'one pole of society in the shape of capital, while at the other pole are grouped masses of men who have nothing to sell but their labour-power' (Marx, 1867a: 899).

This polarization presupposes a very wide conception of the working class, consistent with Engels's clarificatory definition in the 1888 edition of the *Communist Manifesto*:

> By proletariat [is meant] the class of modern wage labourers who, having no means of production of their own, are reduced to selling their labour-power in order to live. (Marx and Engels, 1848: 67 n12)

That conception is consistent with the rest of the *Manifesto* and with Marx's statements elsewhere. The 'modern working class' are described as 'a class of labourers, who live only so long as they find work, and who find work only so long as their labour increases capital' (Marx and Engels, 1848: 73). In *Capital* Marx says: 'The capital-relation presupposes a complete separation between the workers and the ownership of the conditions for the realization of their labour' (Marx, 1867a: 874). Again:

> 'Proletarian' must be understood to mean, economically speaking, nothing other than 'wage labourer', the man who produces and valorizes 'capital', and is thrown onto the street as soon as he becomes superfluous to the need for valorization possessed by 'Monsieur Capital' . . .' (Marx, 1867a: 764 n1).[5]

The importance of being *compelled* to sell one's labour-power is also stressed (*ibid.*: 272).

Engels's clarification is vulnerable to various criticisms. Elster calls on Marx's own comments in the last chapter of *Capital*, vol. 3 (cf. 2.3) to argue that we cannot define class in terms of degrees of ownership and non-ownership of labour-power and means of production: infinite degrees are possible, and this would lead to an infinite fragmentation of classes (Elster, 1985: 322, 1986b: 143). Cohen has argued that being forced to sell one's labour-power does not successfully distinguish people normally taken to be members of the proletariat. Such people are in an objective position no different from, for example, immigrants who arrive penniless but by a mixture of savings and borrowings are able to become small shopkeepers (Cohen, 1986: 240–41). It is not true of the immigrants that they are forced to sell their labour-power, so it is not true of others either. Przeworski entertains similar thoughts. Classes are not a given, but 'historically contingent products of reciprocal actions' (Przeworski, 1985: 96). Proletarians make choices in the light of their goals and resources. A choice to sell one's labour-power is that of an individual not antecedently describable as a worker. The description becomes apposite only as a result of that choice. In that case, membership of the working class cannot be defined in terms of being forced into a certain relation (*ibid*.: 95–7).

Engels's clarification can be protected against these and other objections by the following, more nuanced, definition:

> *By proletariat is meant the modern class of wage- or salary-earning people whose lack of ownership of sufficiently significant means of production results in their having to offer their labour-power for sale, for a significant proportion of their lives,*[6] *if they are to live at an average, reasonable standard of living in the prevailing historical circumstances without engaging in specifiably exceptional or dangerous alternative activities, as well as people who are, in specifiable ways, directly dependent for their own livelihood on members of the proletariat as defined.*

This refurbished definition is proof against technically correct but relatively minor objections. For example, suppose that I own a spade (but nothing else). Then, since a spade is a means of producing wealth, it might be objected that no one who owns a spade is a member of the proletariat. Contrariwise, suppose that every six months I had to sell my labour-power for ten minutes. Then it might be objected that this relatively minor irritation would be enough to categorize me as a proletarian. Having such a light irritation is few people's lot in the world as it is, and Marx and Engels form their conceptions in the first instance to cope with the world as it is rather than as it could conceivably be. The additional qualification regarding a significant period of time makes that clear.

The definition conforms to Marx's basic idea of class in being in one sense 'objective': whether you belong to a particular class depends on the relations you stand in to other human beings and to inanimate objects, rather than on your perceptions or your consciousness. But it also involves questions of quantification and evaluation, rather than the mere recognition of brute facts. (How much is significant? What constitutes a reasonable standard of living? What constitute dangerous activities?) In that respect the definition is indeterminate but perfectly determinable. There may be a grey area in fixing who belongs to the proletariat, but provided that many people fall clearly on each side of the divide, this is not a serious problem.

The original claim about being forced to sell one's labour-power now becomes elliptical. It is not a matter of being forced in an absolute sense, but of having to if one is to achieve certain ends in a certain way. Hence it is compatible with being a proletarian in this sense that one should be described as *choosing* to sell one's labour-power, as Przeworski suggests. No one has to. They could starve, rifle through garbage cans, rob banks, or live off social security. But *if* they want to live a reasonably average life, then they must choose to sell their energies in the absence of large reserves of wealth.[7]

The refurbished definition avoids the language of coercion, which is likely to be accompanied, rightly or wrongly, by the thought that someone is to blame for that coercion. (Marx rejects that view; cf. 4.4.) It distinguishes workers by reference to a causal notion, their non-ownership of the means of production being causally responsible for their need to sell their labour-power if a given state is to be enjoyed. The modal aspect of the definition, however, is important. Membership of this class does not rest on whether one works but on whether one *has to* in order to live in a certain way.

Capitalists are defined in Engels's clarification as 'owners of the means of social production and employers of wage labour' (Marx and Engels, 1848: 67 n12). This definition also requires elaboration to protect it against minor objections. The United Kingdom's General Household Survey for 1987 revealed that just over 20 per cent of the adult population owned shares, a third of them doing so on a weekly income before tax of £100 or less. That would not establish that 20 per cent were capitalists. The ownership of some small quantity of shares no more makes such individuals into capitalists than a cut on the finger makes someone into an invalid. Ownership of the means of production must be significant. How significant? The reasonable and symmetrical answer is: so significant that one can enjoy an average standard of living, etc., from the proceeds of capital investment and without the need to sell one's labour-power.

With these definitions, the resulting anatomy of society differs markedly not only from those standardly employed by many non-Marxists, but also from what would normally be associated with Marx. It differs from those in the Weberian tradition, which present gradations along different dimensions such as wealth and authority. It differs from class analyses based on occupational role, where the group of individuals rich enough not to need an occupation may just disappear from view altogether. But it also differs from an anatomy focusing on industrial, manual workers, as separate from and opposed to other sections of society.[8] The proletariat is here defined in relatively abstract structural terms, and a wider range of individuals will meet that structural requirement than on other definitions.

Marx's view, even when it is refurbished, may seem wholly crude and inadequate. The capitalist class, on this definition, is so tiny as to be insignificant; the working class is far too wide. In that spirit, Wright argues that the conception of workers as wage-earners cannot provide 'a satisfactory structural basis for explaining class formation, class consciousness and class struggle': it 'does not create a category which is in any meaningful sense homogeneous with respect to its effects' (Wright, 1985: 39). In the background here is what Wright terms 'the embarrassment of the middle classes' (ibid.: 13). The idea of polarization in capitalism is no longer generally accepted, because of 'the growth of professional and technical occupations and the expansion of managerial hierarchies in large corporations and the state' (ibid.: 8). To suggest that society really is polarized and that the middle class is an ideological illusion, according to Wright, 'deals with the problem of the middle class by denying the problem itself' (Wright, 1986: 115). He adds (correctly): 'Relatively few theorists have adopted this stance' (ibid.).

Marx does not share the embarrassment. He laments the way the bourgeoisie 'has converted the physician, the lawyer, the priest, the poet, the man of science, into its paid wage labourers' (Marx and Engels, 1848: 70), describes managers[9] as wage labourers (Marx, 1867a: 450), and teachers and writers as productive workers. If a teacher enriches a school-owner, 'That the latter has laid out his capital in a teaching factory, instead of a sausage factory, makes no difference to the relation' (Marx, 1867a: 644; cf. 1905–10: I: 292, 1933: 1044). Whereas Milton wrote as part of his nature, 'the writer who turns out stuff for his publisher in factory style, is a *productive labourer*', and the same would be true for a singer (Marx, 1905–10: I: 401; original emphasis).

Marx does, of course, concentrate on factory workers proper in his discussions, but that is reasonable where they constitute the commonest instantiation of the structural properties defining the working class. As he explains:

if our historical sketch has shown the prominent part played by modern industry ... [it] is still for us only a particular department of the exploitation of labour. (Marx, 1867a: 411)

Service industries are ignored because they 'are of microscopic significance when compared with the mass of capitalist production' (Marx, 1933: 1044–5). Where that is true, such neglect is similarly reasonable.

We should certainly not reject Marx's conception of the working class because it diverges from more familiar conceptions. His theories are theories for revolutionary change, which depend crucially on challenging and changing people's ordinary, non-revolutionary perceptions of the nature of the society they live in. If we also recall the multiplicity of roles which class plays in his thinking (see 2.3), it is not clear that the conception falls to Wright's criticisms. For example, the original polarization claim is plausible on this conception, and will form part of an adequate diagnosis of capitalist social relations. It is probably true that more and more of the population have gravitated to one or other of the two classes as defined. That is, various kinds of independent producers and people of independent means have tended to disappear, and the wage relation has become more dominant. The number of people who can live off investment of capital is relatively small, the number who either must enter a wage or salary contract or are directly dependent on those who must is massive. This justifies Marx's description of the proletariat as 'the immense majority' (Marx and Engels, 1848: 78). Of course, it is not true that the immense majority are manual or factory workers, but then that is not Marx's claim.

Some plausibility also attaches to the implicit claim about the progressive nature of that polarization, as in the statement that 'every fresh development of the productive powers of labour must tend to deepen social contrasts and point social antagonisms' (Marx, 1864: 77–8). Impoverishment is a relative notion for Marx. He offers an analogy. A house shrinks if a palace springs up beside it; similarly, the enjoyments of a worker may rise, but their social satisfaction, their satisfaction relative to what a capitalist can enjoy, may *fall* (Marx, 1849: 93–4). This explains Marx's relatively muted enthusiasm for higher wages, which constitute '*better payment for the slave*, and would not conquer either for the worker or for labour their human status and dignity' (Marx, 1932: 81; original emphasis). He reinforces this in *Capital*, insisting that 'in proportion as capital accumulates, the situation of the worker, *be his payment high or low*, must grow worse' (Marx, 1867a: 799;

emphasis added). As the productivity of labour increases, both capitalist and worker may be able to appropriate greater means of subsistence, but 'in relative terms ... the abyss between the life-situation of the worker and that of the capitalist would keep widening' (*ibid.*: 659; cf. *ibid.*: 806). The productive mechanisms of capitalism ensure that it is 'a system of slavery, increasing in severity commensurately with the development of the social productive forces of labour, *irrespective of whether the worker is then better or worse paid*' (Marx, 1875: 352; emphasis added).

These passages indicate that Marx did not believe that workers must remain at the level of absolute wretchedness which he witnessed in nineteenth-century England, or that they could not increase their material well-being as compared with some earlier time. His prognosis would be false if he did. His point about relative wealth is not so obviously false. Given the accumulation of fortunes among the capitalist class as defined, it may well be that the gap between them and members of the working class as defined has widened.

Moreover, these passages suggest that Marx's concern is not confined to material wealth and poverty. The lot of the worker must grow *worse*, whether more impoverished or not. It is 'the mass of misery, oppression, slavery, degradation and exploitation' which grows (Marx, 1867a: 929). Claims about overall wealth and poverty are complex enough; but these claims are wider and vaguer. Consequently, it will be more difficult either to establish or to refute them. Conceptual clarification is necessary before it is possible to pronounce on them with certainty.

Class in special theory has both diagnostic and normative relevance. To aspire to live in average conditions for one's historical period is nothing if not an average aspiration, and information about what relations someone must enter into in order to achieve it can hardly be irrelevant to where their interests lie. This information will be doubly relevant to their interests. Rational agents *ipso facto* have an interest in retaining control over their lives, and a level of material security and well-being is a precondition for engaging in any further activities or projects (cf. 2.1). The class definitions indicate the price people must pay for furthering any other life plans they have. They therefore designate material interests both *qua* material interests and *qua* preconditions for furthering other interests.

No human being can give their life a chosen shape without attending to the satisfaction of their basic material needs. For some human beings, the relations they must enter into for that satisfaction themselves crucially determine the shape their life does take. Marx holds, justifiably, that the portion of life which a worker loses, as well as the unchosen conditions of life during that portion when they are working for another, is significant enough to carry implications for their fundamental interests. To meet their material needs and to further other projects, they have to enter into relations which have, as their result, that they make over to someone else the right to call on many of their waking hours in tasks which they do not themselves designate. Within such a condition, there may be many varying degrees of material reward[10] and autonomy while working, and these are by any standards significant matters. But they are not as fundamental as the fact of falling into this category in the first place – if only because these differences arise only for those who do fall into this category in the first place.

This further explains why Marx makes the division in society where he does. Capitalists may be numerically insignificant, but the characteristic they possess is highly significant. In capitalism 'the landowner can behave in relation to the land just as any commodity owner can with his commodities', and 'can spend his entire life in Constantinople, while his landed property remains in Scotland' (Marx, 1894: 753, 755). In this way capitalists provide an exemplar. Their projects do not depend on forfeiting large portions of their life in order to find the material prerequisites for furthering them. They stand in qualitative contrast with those who are so dependent.

The diagnostic and normative roles played by class in special theory partly meet Wright's earlier criticisms. Even if the definitions discussed cannot figure in an explanation of class consciousness, they can be used in establishing the claim that class conflict is present in capitalist society. I suggested in 3.3 that for Marx class conflict need not be conscious: those locked in conflict may have no particular feelings about each other *or themselves*, and their hostility may be channelled in quite other directions. There may still be unconscious conflict in this polarization.

The criticism that the definitions of class cannot figure in an explanation of class consciousness is more plausible, but also less damaging (cf. 3.3). They may do little to explain political movements or the ideology people adopt, but we must bear in mind Marx's revolutionary aspirations. If these definitions carry the implications which Marx claims about people's interests, that is a reason for attempting to persuade people to adopt them rather than a reason for abandoning them. The point will be to change their way of looking at themselves. Marx's conception is not shown to be inapposite or outmoded merely because people do not (primarily) take their political identification from it. Crudely, if the point is that they *should*, he is not refuted by showing that they *don't*.

4.3   The Working-Class Collective

Resistance to the stark polarization of 4.2 may remain, reinforced by considerations internal to Marx's own theories. In his general theory, we were told that exploitation consisted in the non-owners of the means of production working additional time to provide for the subsistence of the owners (cf. 3.3). Surely, this division is not captured in the polarization? Marx himself says: 'the extraordinary increase in the productivity of large-scale industry ... permits a larger and larger part of the working class to be employed unproductively' (Marx, 1867a: 574; cf. 1905–10: III: 363). Indeed, he refers to 'the constantly growing number of the middle classes, those who stand between the workman on the one hand and the capitalist and landlord on the other' and 'maintain themselves to an ever increasing extent directly out of revenue' (Marx, 1905–10: II: 573, cited by Nicolaus, 1967: 45). That, surely, provides the reason for rejecting the polarization? Among all those who are proletarian according to the definition in 4.2, many benefit from the additional work discharged by the much narrower band who produce the wealth. These two bands, whose interests differ and even conflict, must be distinguished.

At least two rejoinders are possible. The first concedes that being productive and being under a compulsion to sell one's labour-power denote distinct (though overlapping) groups with associated interests. But, it continues, a conflict of interests between producers and non-producers is no different from and no more fundamental than a clash between different kinds of producer. (Think of the interests of gas and coal producers when it comes to decisions on fuel policy.) Hence, it concludes, there may still be a fundamental shared interest among producing and non-producing workers as defined in 4.2.

The second rejoinder challenges received notions of productivity, just as received notions of working-class membership were challenged. It refines the notion of productiveness to include many who would not normally be so regarded. Marx's comments on the distinction between productive and unproductive labour are ambiguous, occurring mainly in works he did not himself see through the press (principally *Theories of Surplus-Value* and *Capital*, vols 2 and 3). However, the second rejoinder, derivable from what he says in published work (notably *Capital*, vol. 1), sits more comfortably with his other theoretical commitments.[11]

Marx begins his special theory with the idea of individual human beings working on material, to produce an object for exchange against some other object. Concentration on that basic activity leads some commentators to equate the realm of productive activity with the manual transformation of natural matter, explicitly excluding the production of non-material goods (e.g. Mandel, 1978: 43; Shaw, 1978: 33). But Marx begins from this basic case in order to show that its simplicity is deceptive: complicated social relations necessarily grow up around it.

> Capitalist production destroys the basis of commodity production in so far as the latter involves independent individual production and the exchange of commodities between owners or the exchange of equivalents. (Marx, 1933: 951)

The producing entity is no longer the individual but the *collective worker*. The product is no longer (necessarily) a material object but *surplus-value*.

Recall that the starting point of capitalist production, according to Marx, is the gathering of a large number of workers in one place (Marx, 1867a: 439). Their co-operation brings about a crucial change. Just as the offensive power of a squadron is essentially different from the sum of offensive powers of the individual soldiers, so the social force created when many hands co-operate differs from the sum total of forces exerted by separate individuals. A new, intrinsically collective, productive power is created (*ibid.*: 443). The collective worker is formed from the combination of many specialized workers (*ibid.*: 464), and the excellence it displays occurs at the expense of the individual workers: their imperfections or one-sidedness become virtues and many-sided excellence for it (*ibid.*: 468–9):

> In manufacture, the social productive power of the collective worker, hence of capital, is enriched through the impoverishment of the worker in individual productive power. (*ibid.*: 483)

There is a crucial accompanying shift in the conception of productive labour and the productive labourer.

The product is transformed from the direct product of the individual producer into a social product, the joint product of a collective labourer, i.e. a combination of workers, each of whom stands at a different distance from the actual manipulation of the object of labour. (*ibid.*: 643)

In order to work productively, it is no longer necessary for the individual himself to put his hand to the object; it is sufficient for him to be an organ of the collective labourer, and to perform any one of its subordinate functions. (*ibid.*: 643–4)

Productive activity as manipulation of material 'is derived from the nature of material production itself, and it remains correct for the collective labourer considered as a whole. But it no longer holds good for each member taken individually' (*ibid.*: 644; cf. 1905–10: I: 411–12).

Marx then argues: 'Capitalist production is not merely the production of commodities, it is, by its very essence, the production of surplus-value' (Marx, 1867a: 644). The use of money as capital, to make more money or increase value, also changes the range of those who might be regarded as productive:

The only worker who is productive is one who produces surplus-value for the capitalist, or in other words contributes towards the self-valorization of capital. (*ibid.*; cf. 1905–10: I: 156–7)

If the main goal of economic activity in capitalism is increase in value rather than the production of objects, this explains why Marx is unembarrassed by the thought of schoolteachers being productive.[12] It also explains why there is no problem in extending his analysis to cover service industry, where it assumes greater significance.

As the image of a lone individual, working on raw material and transforming it, is inapposite as an image of modern, large-scale production, it becomes not merely difficult in practice but misconceived in principle to attempt to calculate whether an individual is a net producer of surplus-value. Here is one reason why. Even in the simplest case, in order to know how much value was added to a commodity by a given labourer we should need to separate that labourer's contribution from two other factors: the quantity of value transferred to the commodity from the means of production which the labourer uses, and the value of the commodity before that labourer began to work on it (Marx, 1867a: 293–4). The calculation of the commodity's value at that earlier stage would depend on the same considerations, and so on back to the stage when the raw materials making up the commodity were mined from the earth. Even there the same recursive problem would arise: calculation of how much value was added to the raw material specifically by the labourer would depend on how much value was transferred to it from the instruments used to mine it, and so on.

Marx observes that 'the specialized worker produces no commodities. It is only the common product of all the specialized workers that becomes a commodity' (*ibid.*: 475), and approvingly quotes Thomas Hodgskin:

> There is no longer anything which we can call the natural reward of individual labour. Each labourer produces only some part of a whole, and each part, having no value or utility in itself, there is nothing on which the labourer can seize, and say: It is my product, this I will keep to myself. (*ibid.*: 475 n34)

According to Marx, the 'labour expended on each commodity can no longer be calculated – except as an average, i.e. an ideal estimate' (Marx, 1933: 954).

Individuals can be described as 'productive' derivatively, by virtue of their combination into a unit which can itself be so described. Their productiveness consists in their contributing positively to *the collective's* production of surplus-value, their performing *any* of its subordinate tasks.[13] Such derivative attributions are then explicitly removed from any idea of manual labour. Included among productive workers 'are all those who contribute in one way or another to the production of the commodity, from the actual operative to the manager or engineer' (Marx, 1905–10: I: 156–7). When one individual works on an object there is no separate supervisory role, no distinction between mental and physical labour, whereas in the case of the collective worker specialization requires that. An industrial army

> requires, like a real army, officers (managers) and N.C.O.s (foremen, overseers) who command during the labour process in the name of capital. The work of supervision becomes their established and exclusive function. (Marx, 1867a: 450)

They become 'a special kind of wage labourer' (*ibid.*).

Productiveness in this sense requires varying conditions of existence and material reward, on Marx's premisses:

> Since the various functions performed by the collective worker can be simple or complex, high or low, the individual labour-powers, his organs, require different degrees of training, and must therefore possess very different values. Manufacture therefore develops a hierarchy of labour-powers, to which there corresponds a scale of wages. (*ibid.*: 469)

However, this position contradicts a view expressed earlier:

> The various interests and conditions of life within the ranks of the proletariat are more and more equalized, in proportion as machinery obliterates all distinctions of labour, and nearly everywhere reduces wages to the same low level. (Marx and Engels, 1848: 75)

The practical importance of this is taken up in 5.3.

The collective worker constitutes a collective as outlined in 2.4. It possesses powers which its constituent parts could not possess, and the significance of those constituents can be expressed only by ineliminable reference to the collective. The gains which accrue from co-operation, for example, are additional to anything individuals *qua* individuals can achieve:

> The combined working day produces a greater quantity of use-values than an equal sum of isolated working days ... the special productive power of the combined working day is, under all circumstances, the social productive power of labour ... This power arises from co-operation itself. (Marx, 1867a: 447)

This is important to the capitalist, who pays 'the value of 100 independent labour-powers, but he does not pay for the combined labour-power of the 100' (*ibid.*: 451). The additional power which is provided by the collective as such 'develops as a free gift to capital' (*ibid.*).

The shift of focus from the individual to the collective worker suggests a wide construal of the collective worker itself (although this is inexplicit in Marx's text). Calculation of individuals' contribution to surplus-value in the individual firm is not possible because we cannot sub-divide the collective effort resulting in surplus-value. But the same is true of the contribution of the individual firm to the sum total of surplus-value. Many inputs into the total surplus-value will lie outside the limits set by the firm. Workers as diverse as doctors, social workers and housewives may, in Marx's words, contribute towards the self-valorization of capital – their presence and effort being a necessary condition of the realization of that increase in value. This suggests a move to the level of considering the total workforce as responsible for the total surplus-value created: at its widest, the entire working population of the capitalist system. The importance of that possibility for Marx's practical project will become apparent in Chapter 5.[14]

We see now a further reason for not rejecting Marx's definition of the working class in 4.2. We cannot justifiably do that before considering his argument that those gathered under this concept have a further, less obvious characteristic in common: they are members of an invisible collective, all contributing to a state of affairs of whose existence they may not even be aware without the equipment Marx's own theory provides. The problem for Marx, however, is that this claim is itself open to two complementary challenges: that not *all* workers are productive, even in the extended sense of contributing to the production and realization of surplus-value; and that not *only* they do so.

In connection with the first challenge, Przeworski suggests that we should not 'jump into the abyss of functionalism', seeing everything that happens as necessary for reproducing capitalist relations (Przeworski, 1985: 85). We can be fairly confident that surplus-value would not be created and realized without attendant efforts of doctors and educators, for example. But does every single person who has to sell their labour-power end up performing tasks essential to the system? Even if that unqualified claim is not true, however, some related claim may be, to the effect that the overwhelming number of workers by the criterion originally laid down are also involved, directly or indirectly, in activities which are themselves indispensable to the system based on production of surplus-value. Marx might then draw on the first rejoinder mentioned at the beginning of this section, and attempt to link these people with other workers not so involved by reference to a more fundamental shared interest arising from their common wage-labouring condition.

However, the second challenge asserts that this is not true only of workers. Some capitalists choose to work, and are part of the collective worker. Marx himself says that capital 'is a collective product, and ... only by the united action of all members of society, can it be set in motion' (Marx and Engels,

1848: 81). Marx's wisest course is to concede this challenge but limit its damage. We shall see in 5.2 the unique role he assigns to the working class in the transformation of society, but his case does not depend on any one feature distinguishing them from others. To contribute to the production and realization of surplus-value where one is *constrained* to enter into the relations having that result is quite different from doing so out of choice. Similarly, to contribute to that end when the surplus-value so produced belongs to others is quite different from doing so when it accrues to oneself. In both respects workers differ from capitalists. Moreover, Marx is entitled to add that the capitalist does not work for the production of surplus-value *qua* capitalist:

> Capitalist production has itself brought it about that the work of supervision is readily available, quite independent of the ownership of capital. It has therefore become superfluous for this work of supervision to be performed by the capitalist. (Marx, 1894: 511)

And he cites approvingly Andrew Ure's remark: 'it is not the industrial capitalists but rather the industrial managers who are "the soul of our industrial system".' (*ibid.*: 510)

4.4 Exploitation in Special Theory

Marx believes that many inevitable features of commodity society deeply and adversely affect the interests of the working class – for example, periodic crises and unemployment. It might, indeed, be felt that history has done little to disprove that part of his case. But he claims more strongly that, even without these features, capitalism would be unacceptable. This follows from the intrinsic nature of capitalist exploitation. We saw in 3.3 that Marx characterized exploitation as the extraction of surplus labour from subordinate classes. The historically specific form this takes in capitalism resurrects the idea, familiar from synchronic materialism, of the need to penetrate appearances to a reality which lies beneath.

Capitalist exploitation developed out of feudal exploitation (Marx, 1867a: 875), but differs crucially from it. The feudal *corvée* 'presents surplus labour in an independent and immediately perceptible form' (*ibid.*: 345). The worker in capitalism also performs surplus labour, but 'this fact is not directly visible' (*ibid.*). The object bought and sold in the central transaction of capitalist

society is not labour but labour-*power*, the *ability* to labour, 'the
aggregate of those mental and physical capabilities existing in the
physical form, the living personality . . . whenever he produces a
use-value of any kind' (*ibid*.: 270).

> When we speak of capacity for labour, we do not speak of labour, any
> more than we speak of digestion when we speak of capacity for
> digestion. As is well known, the latter process requires something more
> than a good stomach. (*ibid*.: 277; cf. *ibid*.: 678)

The analogy indicates why the distinction matters to Marx. In
order to digest, as opposed to merely having the capacity for
digestion, I must have access to appropriate material. Similarly:

> In order that a man may be able to sell commodities other than his
> labour-power, he must of course possess means of production, such as
> raw materials, instruments of labour, etc. (*ibid*.: 272)

But workers do not, so they cannot exercise their labour-power,
they cannot labour, and they cannot sell their labour.

> In order to be sold as a commodity in the market, labour must at all
> events exist before it is sold. But if the worker were able to endow it
> with an independent existence, he would be selling a commodity, and
> not labour. (*ibid*.: 675)

Instead, workers must sell their capacity to labour. They labour,
but after – and as a consequence of – their contract.

When labour-power is bought from the worker by the capitalist,
the capitalist acquires the use of it. The capacity is actualized, the
worker works, on raw materials which have also been bought by
the capitalist. During one part of the labour-process the worker
produces value equivalent to the value which went into producing
their labour-power, but when they are no longer merely replacing
the value which was required to purchase their capacity, they
produce surplus-value for the capitalist. Part of their effort goes
into labour necessary for their own needs and part goes into
surplus labour. The ratio of surplus labour to necessary labour, or
surplus-value to necessary value, 'is therefore an exact expression
of the degree of exploitation of labour-power by capital, or of the
worker by the capitalist' (*ibid*.: 326). The capitalist is thus able to

purchase 'a commodity whose use-value possesses the peculiar property of being a source of value' (*ibid.*: 270).

We now see why theoretical clarification is needed if we are to understand the nature of capitalist exploitation. The division of the day into necessary and surplus labour is disguised. The worker receives a wage for the integrated day, so that it looks as though all labour is paid labour. This differs from feudalism:

> The necessary labour which the Wallachian peasant performs for his own maintenance is distinctly marked off from his surplus labour on behalf of the boyar. The one he does on his own field, the other on the seignorial estate. (*ibid.*: 346; cf. *ibid.*: 680)

By contrast, 'the money-relation conceals the uncompensated labour of the wage labourer': it 'makes the actual relation invisible' (*ibid.*: 680). The special nature of labour-power 'falls outside the frame of reference of the everyday consciousness' (*ibid.*: 681), since the 'forms of appearance are reproduced directly and spontaneously, as current and usual modes of thought' (*ibid.*: 682). Consequently, 'the essential relation must first be discovered by science' (*ibid.*).

There is a further contrast. Serfs are coerced into making payments in kind, and working on another's property for a period after working on their own. There is not the same kind of coercion in the capitalist relation. Workers are free to make a contract with capitalists (*ibid.*: 272). This surface freedom, however, once again conceals a deeper truth. Since the contract must be entered into if the worker's needs are to be met, 'the period of time for which he is free to sell his labour-power is the period of time for which he is forced to sell it' (*ibid.*: 415). Those 'who have nothing to sell but their labour-power ... are compelled to sell themselves voluntarily' (*ibid.*: 899). That is a different matter from straightforward coercion. Marx says, 'The silent compulsion of economic relations sets the seal on the domination of the capitalist over the worker' (*ibid.*). The necessity arises causally from what has to be done in order to achieve an average standard of living (cf. 4.2).

Relations of exploitation clearly have vastly different consequences for worker and capitalist. For the worker they 'transform his life-time into working-time' (*ibid.*: 799), and work itself is 'just effort and torment' (Marx, 1933: 989). A significant portion of life is therefore taken away; it assumes a shape and a character beyond the control of the person whose life it is (or was, before the sale of labour-power). Moreover, the workers cement themselves into these relations in the very process of exploitation itself, which 'incessantly converts material wealth into capital, into the capitalist's means of enjoyment and his means of valorization' (Marx, 1867a: 716). But they always themselves leave that process in the same state as they entered it: 'a personal source of wealth, but deprived of any means of making that wealth a reality' for themselves (*ibid.*). They reproduce a system that leaves them separated from the resources which are a precondition of their living a life not dominated by the sale of labour-power and its consequences. Their particular circumstances may vary, for example, with rises or falls in wage levels, but any rise is

> confined within limits that not only leave intact the foundations of the capitalist system, but also secure its reproduction on an increasing scale. . . . It cannot be otherwise in a mode of production in which the worker exists to satisfy the need of the existing values for valorization, as opposed to the inverse situation, in which objective wealth is there to satisfy the worker's own need for development. (*ibid.*: 772)

By contrast, capitalists have control of what they have bought, and that implies control over the worker in whom their purchase inheres. Labour 'belongs to the capitalist as a substance that creates and increases wealth' (Marx, 1933: 990). Since the surplus-value, the additional capital created by labour, is the source of the capitalist's privileged position, it is in their interest 'to receive as much labour as possible for as little money as possible' (*ibid.*: 682). There is therefore an 'unavoidable antagonism' between the exploiter and the raw material of his exploitation' (*ibid.*: 449).

Historically, privileged classes could follow cultural and other pursuits because labouring classes provided for their material needs. Capitalism has given rise to a technology which would obviate the need for some to live at the expense of others in this way. It has developed at a massive rate and promises 'the general reduction of the necessary labour of society to a minimum, which then corresponds to the artistic, scientific etc. development of the individuals in the time set free, and with the means created, for all of them' (Marx, 1939: 706). The effort which has to go into providing for material needs could be minimized, and people could live lives of their own choosing, freed from this material burden. The achievements of capitalism make it no longer necessary for some to live at the expense of others' efforts.

But the demands of capitalism prevent the realization of this potential. It 'diminishes labour-time in the necessary form so as to increase it in the superfluous form' (*ibid.*). Whereas 'in any economic formation of society where the use-value rather than the exchange-value of the product predominates, surplus labour will be restricted by a more or less confined set of needs', in capitalism a 'boundless thirst for surplus labour will arise from the character of production itself' (Marx, 1867a: 345). The capitalist's control, therefore, is only mediate. He or she is under a compulsion from the overriding imperative of the system: the creation and accumulation of more and more surplus in the form of capital.

The subject of exploitation in capitalism is an invisible collective producing surplus-value. Exploitation is not confined to those who manually produce objects, nor to those producing the means of subsistence. On the contrary, the greater a society's productivity, the greater will be the number of people released from producing subsistence and made 'available for exploitation in other spheres' (Marx, 1894: 921). Nor will the polarized relations between capitalist and worker always appear in that guise. Conflicts *within* the collective worker may be perceived more easily than those between it and the capitalist class. Equally, the exploitative process itself may be obscured by the interposition of a hierarchy, as in the case of piece wages where 'the exploitation of the worker by capital takes place through the medium of the exploitation of one worker by another' (Marx, 1867a: 695). The basic clash – between classes as defined in 4.2 – is obscured, intermediaries in the hierarchy of exploitation are perceived as the main enemy, and capitalists proper may disappear from consciousness altogether. Yet members of the collective worker may have reason to form an alliance with the immediately perceived extractor of surplus-value in order to put an end to the process of surplus-extraction altogether.

The existence of exploitation is obviously supposed to function as a reason for abolishing capitalism. This has led many commentators to claim that Marx's conception of exploitation is an implicitly moral one, carrying connotations of injustice. Since his explicit attitude to morality and justice is scathing, it is paradoxical if he needs to employ those categories in his critique of capitalism.

He criticizes Proudhon for seeking to reform the commodity system in accordance with an ideal of justice (Marx, 1867a: 178 n2), and describes law, morality and religion as 'so many bourgeois prejudices, behind which lurk in ambush just as many bourgeois interests' (Marx and Engels, 1848: 78). In the *Critique of the Gotha Programme* he comments:

When the class struggle is rejected as a disagreeable 'coarse' phenomenon, nothing remains as the basis of socialism other than 'true love of
humanity' and empty phrases about 'justice'. (Marx, 1875: 373)

He says at least once in published writings that the extraction of a
surplus from the worker involves no injustice. The seller of labour-
power, like any other commodity-seller, relinquishes the use of
what is sold; its buyer acquires the use of it, and 'this circumstance
is a piece of good luck for the buyer, but by no means an injustice
towards the seller' (Marx, 1867a: 301). The labour-process occurs
with things which belong to the capitalist, and 'the product of this
process belongs to him just as much as the wine which is the
product of the process of fermentation going on in his cellar' (*ibid.*:
292).

According to Marx, the worker furnishes surplus-value 'without
having the fair price of his commodity cut by even a farthing'
(*ibid.*: 732). The whole product, including the surplus, 'becomes
the legitimate property of the capitalist' (*ibid.*). Indeed:

The time during which the worker works is the time during which the
capitalist consumes the labour-power he has bought from him. If the
worker consumes his disposable time for himself, he robs the capitalist.
(*ibid.*: 342)

In posthumous writings, the stronger claim occurs that this
relation is positively just: 'The justice of transactions between
agents of production consists in the fact that these transactions
arise from the relations of production as their natural consequence', and their 'content is just so long as it corresponds to the
mode of production and is adequate to it' (Marx, 1894: 460–61).

What is the counter-evidence, to suggest that Marx did think
capitalist exploitation unjust? In the unpublished *Grundrisse* he
says that labour's 'recognition of the products as its own, and the
judgement that its separation from the conditions of its realization
is improper [*ungehörig*] – forcibly imposed – is an enormous
[advance in] awareness', and in a subsequent manuscript he
replaces 'ungehörig' with 'ein Unrecht' – an injustice (Marx, 1939:
463, cited by Elster, 1985: 106 and Lukes, 1985: 51 n1). In his
published work he frequently alludes to the theft or robbery
involved in capitalist exploitation. He likens it to 'the age-old
activity of the conqueror who buys commodities from the
conquered with the money he has stolen from them' (Marx, 1867a:
728). He refers to the 'constant appropriation by the capitalist,

without equivalent, of a portion of the labour of others' (*ibid*.: 730) and 'the unpaid labour of [the capitalist's] workers' (*ibid*.: 732). Most explicitly, he implies that capitalism involves 'robbing' the worker (*ibid*.: 638) and describes the surplus as being 'embezzled' from the worker (*ibid*.: 761).

This contradictory evidence has prompted a range of interpretations: that Marx thought capitalist exploitation unjust, that he did not think it unjust, that he thought it unjust but did not think he did.[15] A judgement as to whether Marx's critique of capitalist exploitation is based on morality or (a distinct matter) justice will turn on one's conception of morality or justice. Lukes, for example, draws the boundaries of morality so widely that it would be virtually impossible for Marx or any other social theorist to avoid reliance on morality. It includes not merely the domain of the right and the good, but also 'assumptions about the nature of man, the preconditions for social life, the limits of its possible transformation, and the grounds of practical judgment' (Lukes, 1985: 2). Marx's critique, however, departs from a number of common presuppositions of moral and justice-based discourse.

Morality is often understood as a set of demands on individuals, designed to temper how they would behave if left to follow their own inclinations or interests. Its role is to afford protection to *other* individuals in that way. There is then an essential contrast between my own good and the good of others, an appeal to altruism, and a universality and unconditionality attaching to the demands of morality. Individuals' failure to conform to the dictates of morality licenses blame and attributions of specifically moral responsibility.

According to Marx, the communists

> do not preach *morality* at all. . . . They do not put to people the moral demand: love one another, do not be egoists, etc.; on the contrary, they are very well aware that egoism, just as much as self-sacrifice, *is* in definite circumstances a necessary form of the self-assertion of individuals. Hence, the communists by no means want . . . to do away with the 'private individual' for the sake of the 'general', self-sacrificing man. (Marx and Engels, 1932: 267; original emphasis)

In communist society individuals' development is determined by 'the connection of individuals', which is 'the necessary solidarity of the free development of all' (Marx and Engels, 1932: 483).

The individuals' consciousness of their mutual relations will, of course,

likewise become something quite different, and, therefore, will no more
be the 'principle of love' or *dévoûment*, than it will be egoism. (*ibid*.:
483–4)

Marx appeals here to the possibility of practical collective
identification, a type of motivation distinct from the familiar
dichotomy of morality and self-interest (cf. 2.5). The welfare and
interests of collectives to which I belong are in one sense external
to me, but not in the same sense as the interests of some entity of
which I am not a part.

   Nor does Marx's critique exhibit moral impartiality and universality. He sponsors the interests of a particular class, and criticizes
German socialism for ignoring the interests of the proletariat in
favour of

> the interests of human nature, of man in general, who belongs to no
> class, has no reality, who exists only in the misty realm of philosophical
> fantasy. (Marx and Engels, 1848: 91)

It may seem that implicitly Marx does share the moral assumptions. The emancipation of the proletariat is of implicitly universal
significance, since it heralds the emancipation of the whole of
humanity. And if there are morally relevant differences between
classes, then it is an expression of, rather than a departure from,
impartiality to treat them differently.

   Now undoubtedly, Marx shares *some* moral assumptions: he
holds views on what a desirable world might look like. But
impartiality in this weak sense of acting consistently is not a
particular presupposition of morality. He certainly departs from
impartiality in any stronger sense, having 'no scruples about
overthrowing the rule of the bourgeoisie and abolishing its "well-
being" ' (Marx and Engels, 1932: 235).

   Marx also denies that capitalists are morally responsible for
exploitation. Conceding that he does not depict them in rosy
colours, he asserts:

> My standpoint, from which the development of the economic formation
> of society is viewed as a process of natural history, can less than any
> other make the individual responsible for relations whose creature he
> remains, socially speaking, however much he may subjectively raise
> himself above them. (Marx, 1867a: 92)

He speaks of *capital*, rather than capitalists, stealing the time and taking no account of the health and length of life of the worker unless society forces it to do so (*ibid*.: 375–6, 381). This

> does not depend on the will, either good or bad, of the individual capitalist. Under free competition, the immanent laws of capitalist production confront the individual capitalist as a coercive force external to him. (*ibid*.: 381; cf. *ibid*.: 433)

Capitalists, then, suffer coercion, just as workers are compelled to sell their life, but compelled 'by social conditions' rather than by culpable human agencies (*ibid*.: 382). The capitalist's desire to acquire exchange-values is 'the effect of a social mechanism in which he is merely a cog' (*ibid*.: 739). Marx's condemnation of exploitation does not, therefore, rest on the principle that 'people should get what they deserve' and that 'people are responsible (at most) for their intentions' (Arneson, 1981: 205). Talk of desert and responsibility is just what Marx eschews.

Such an eschewal is compatible with the shift from individual to class perspective. That shift enables us to perceive the collective worker and its achievements, as well as the relations in which individual workers stand to the capitalist class as a whole (cf. 4.3 n15). It enables Marx to generate further claims about how *interests* are affected by exploitation, for which he does not need the common presuppositions of morality. Those claims involve, moreover, not only collective interests in the colloquial sense of interests shared by individuals in a common condition, but also the interests *of a collective itself* in the way described in 2.5. Workers do share common interests *qua* individual workers, but their practical deliberation should include consideration of themselves *qua* members of the collective worker, since that is such a central part of what each of them is. They have reason to identify with that corporate entity's interests, and it is itself severely disadvantaged by the appropriation of what it produces, with consequences for its members.

Even if it is not in one's interests to be exploited, no normative conclusion yet follows about what to do. Sale of one's labour-power involves forfeiture of a significant part of one's life, but it would still be an empowering relation, if recompense for doing so leaves one with greater resources in the remainder of one's life than any other feasible arrangement. That, of course, is not Marx's view. He holds that the proletariat has an escape-interest, and posits a specific set of conditions concerning what it has reason to do as a political movement (cf. 5.2).

Marx's critique of exploitation similarly departs from common assumptions about justice. He famously addresses the topic in the *Critique of the Gotha Programme*, criticizing the Programme's demand for 'a just distribution of the proceeds of labour' (Marx, 1875: 343). He is apologetic about dealing at length with the ideas of equal right and just distribution at all,[16] but believes it is necessary so as to avoid being taken in by 'a load of obsolete verbal rubbish' and 'ideological, legal and other humbug' (*ibid.*: 347–8). He asks rhetorically: 'Are economic relations regulated by legal concepts of right or is the opposite not the case?' (*ibid.*: 344). The question is rhetorical because for Marx it is obvious that the answer is the opposite:

> The distribution of the means of consumption at any given time is merely a consequence of the distribution of the conditions of production themselves. (*ibid.*: 348)

His pre-eminent concern with social change leads him to concentrate on the independent rather than the dependent variables in that process.

In the light of this, consider Marx's comments that robbery and embezzlement are involved in exploitation. Robbing is defined in the *Shorter Oxford Dictionary* as depriving someone of something by unlawful force *or* superior power. This mirrors well the distinction between *de jure* and *de facto* ownership (cf. 3.2), and indicates a similar distinction in the case of robbery. It can be specified in a way entirely free of reference to legal or moral notions. Marx's characterization of capitalist exploitation as involving robbery does not, therefore, commit him to the claim that it is unjust. Might there nevertheless be some reason for him to employ the *de jure* sense? When he speaks scathingly of notions of morality and justice, this is on the grounds not of their dubious cognitive status but of their dubious social function in reinforcing existing attitudes and relations. This makes it unlikely that he would employ the *de jure* sense. In normal circumstances it would be entirely inappropriate to confront one's robber with the proposition that they are acting unjustly. Their conduct already shows that they allow that fact no influence on their conduct. There might be marginally more sense in appealing to justice if one were looking to some third party to rescue one from the robber, but for Marx that is not a possible route out of capitalist exploitation (cf. 5.2).

The third possibility is that the robbed, the workers, might need to tell *themselves* that they are the victims of an injustice in order to galvanize themselves into escaping it. But this fails to give due weight to Marx's point about dependent and independent variables:

> To clamour for *equal or even equitable retribution* [*sic*] on the basis of the wages system is the same as to clamour for *freedom* on the basis of the slavery system. What you think just or equitable is out of the question. The question is: What is necessary and unavoidable with a given system of production? (Marx, 1898: 426; original emphasis)

The conception of justice itself arises from misperception of the nature of the exchange between worker and capitalist, and the mistaken notion that it is labour rather than labour-power which is sold:

> All the notions of justice held by both the worker and the capitalist, all the mystifications of the capitalist mode of production . . . have as their basis the form of appearance . . . which makes the actual relation invisible and indeed presents to the eye the precise opposite of that relation. (Marx, 1867a: 680)

It might be objected that Marx's commitment to the causal priority of productive arrangements over distributive ones does not prescind from a concern with just distribution. If the system of production is causally responsible for what I see as unjust distribution, that simply gives me a reason to pursue my concern with justice at the appropriately more basic level of transforming the system of production (cf. Arneson, 1981: 223; Cohen, 1988: 299–300). Indeed, is not Marx himself concerned with distribution, where this includes the 'division of all economic benefits and burdens' (Arneson, 1981: 225; cf. Geras, 1985: 59, Cohen, 1988: 300)? He says:

> The worker's propertylessness and the ownership of living labour by objectified labour . . . are fundamental conditions of the bourgeois mode of production . . . These modes of distribution are the relations of production themselves, but *sub specie distributionis*. (Marx, 1939: 832, cited by Cohen; 1988: 300)

Just as Marx's claims might be seen as moral on a sufficiently wide conception of morality, so they can be construed as distributive if distribution is construed widely enough. But it is

important to see where he diverges from the common presuppositions of justice, and why he couches his own claims *sub specie
productionis*. His primary aim is not a fairer or more equitable
distribution of goods. As we shall see in Chapter 5, he envisages a
change far more radical than that. The literal loss of life
consequent on the need to sell one's labour-power, the central
affliction of the proletariat, is something which cannot be
adequately articulated except by reference to the mode of
production described as such. As regards productive resources
themselves, Marx envisages a form of indivisible collective
ownership which renders talk of equal shares simply inapposite.
He envisages an agency consisting of people who vary greatly
in respect of material wealth to initiate these changes. To bind
them into a force for such change requires attention to be directed
not to the quantitative respect in which they differ but to the
qualitative respect in which they are alike. Their position as
workers, and the constraints this places on their aspirations, is
itself a far broader consideration than merely how well-off they
are.[17]

Marx's departure from common presuppositions of morality and
justice exempts him from certain difficulties. Take the problem of
cleanly generated capitalism (cf. Arneson, 1981: 204–7; Cohen,
1990a: 384–7, 1990b: 30–31; Elster, 1985: 226–9; Nozick, 1974:
160–64). Marx argues that force made possible the primitive
accumulation of wealth from which capitalism began (Marx,
1867a: 874). But suppose things were otherwise. Suppose an initial
fair distribution of assets. Then we may still anticipate that freely
conducted transactions among people with different skills, diligence
and preferences for leisure as against accumulation of goods would
result in some controlling vastly greater resources than others. But
if a population proceeds from an initially just situation through a
series of just steps to a new state of affairs, how can the result be
stigmatized as unjust? The story about forceful dispossession 'does
not impugn capitalism as such. It impugns only capitalisms with
one sort of (dirty) pre-history' (Cohen, 1990b: 30).

That is a serious matter, given Marx's desire to show the
unacceptability of capitalism as such, rather than just some
particular instantiation of it. Or at least it would be, if he wished
to say it was immoral or unjust. He himself emphasizes the
relative unimportance of the genetic question of what brought the
system into being:

. . . in the flood of production the total capital originally advanced becomes a vanishing quantity (*magnitudo evanescens* in the mathematical sense), in comparison with the directly accumulated capital . . . (Marx, 1867a: 734)

He could not do so if he were operating with the common presuppositions of morality and justice, but he can if he is making a claim about where different groups' *interests* lie. I might find myself in a situation which runs counter to my interests even if in reaching that point everyone, including myself, has behaved in a morally impeccable way. The theoretical possibility of cleanly generated capitalism does not, therefore, provide a problem for him.[18]

Notes

1. For their classical statement see Böhm-Bawerk (1896) and Schumpeter (1943), and recent echoings in Nozick (1974: 253–62). Other recent discussion occurs in Roemer (1982a,b, 1989), Steedman (1981) and Wolff (1981, 1984).
2. Commentators standardly note that Marx is influenced by Aristotle's view that there can be no exchange without equality and no equality without commensurability (cf. Marx, 1867a: 151). The difficulty I raise here for his argument echoes a point of Plato's in the famous Third Man Argument of the *Parmenides*, 131E–132B.
3. Commodities imply ownership, of course, but ownership can be defined in terms of *de facto* control, with no reference to legal notions, even if a legal superstructure is necessary to enforce such control (cf. 3.2).
4. It was common enough in academic work, as well as in practical politics, for both sympathizers and opponents of Eastern European regimes to accept their claim to be socialist. For a relatively rare challenge to this self-description, on similar grounds to mine, see Miller (1975: 253).
5. Valorization [*Verwertung*] is the process of increasing value.
6. This refers not to a significant proportion of a person's lifespan, but to a significant proportion of any given period within that span. It is not a necessary condition of being a worker that one has to sell one's labour-power for forty years out of a total of seventy (though that is often the case); rather that, say, in a given week one has to sell one's labour-power for thirty hours rather than two minutes. This amends an error in the definition in Graham (1989a), which had the consequence that no one would be able to tell whether they were a member of the working class until several years of their life had elapsed.
7. It might seem that Cohen's argument shows that no one is forced even

in this elliptical sense. This depends on how we interpret the 'significant period of time' of the refurbished definition. His counter-examples show that someone can on occasion change their class membership, rather than that something ceases to be true of them while they are still a member of a given class. An important element in the escape from the proletarian condition is 'savings . . . accumulated, perhaps painfully, *while still in the proletarian condition'* (Cohen, 1986: 241; emphasis added). But then there *is* a significant period when the escapees have to sell their labour-power, though it may come to an end.

8. Identification of the working class with manual workers occurs in Przeworski (1985: 104) and Poulantzas (1975: 270).

9. 'Manager' is a slippery term, whose application ranges from workers occupying relatively minor supervisory roles to managing directors paid enormous salaries and capitalists who choose to work in their own industry. The first category are likely to be workers on the refurbished definition, but the latter two are not, since their salary is of a level from which it follows that they do not *need* to sell their labour-power for a significant proportion of time in order to enjoy an average standard of living.

10. It is not a consequence of proletarian status, on the refurbished definition, that someone enjoys only an average standard of living. They might *both* have no available alternative means of achieving the average *and* receive remuneration which enabled them to live above the average.

11. Alternative interpretations of Marx restrict, rather than widening, the category of productive labour. He distinguishes between costs and supervision necessary to production in general, in any society, and those necessary only to production of commodities in capitalist society (Marx, 1867a: 448–50, 1894: 507–10, 1905–10: III: 505). Some commentators then suggest that for Marx the only productive work is that associated with the former. But it is not clear why the test for productiveness in an actual society should rest on what would be true of someone in a hypothetical society. Nor does this restriction explain why productiveness should be allied with fundamental interests. Does a cleaner who moves from an unproductive bank to a productive factory acquire different fundamental interests? For helpful discussion see Gough (1972) and Wright (1985: 39–40, 154–73).

12. Mandel argues that it is a basic thesis of *Capital* that 'there can be no production without (concrete) labour, no concrete labour without appropriation and transformation of material objects' (Mandel, 1978: 43), and he asks: 'What is the "immaterial good" produced by a wage-earning teacher . . .?' (*ibid.*: 43 n48). The immediate answer is that the immaterial (though embodied) good which teachers produce is labour-power in various more developed or specialized forms. But the mediate answer, more abstract but more important for Marx's purposes, is that

precisely by producing *that* commodity teachers produce surplus-value.

13. Here I depart from Miliband's interpretation of Marx's claim that one labours productively if one performs one of the subordinate functions of the collective labourer. Miliband construes this as indicating subordination to *other* individual labourers and produces a corresponding conception of the working class confined to those at the lower end of the income scale and 'scale of regard' (Miliband, 1977: 24). Given that Marx's own comments clearly identify those individuals in *super*ordinate positions as themselves labourers, my suggestion is that the position of subordination in Marx's comment contrasts not with the position of other individuals but with the position of the collective labourer itself. Taken in that way, *any* individual worker is subordinate.

14. The capitalist class, too, constitutes a collective *vis-à-vis* individual workers:

> The worker leaves the capitalist to whom he hires himself whenever he likes . . . But the worker, whose sole source of livelihood is the sale or [*sic*] his labour-power, cannot leave the *whole class of purchasers, that is, the capitalist class*, without renouncing his existence. He belongs not to this or that capitalist but to the *capitalist class* . . . (Marx, 1849: 83; original emphasis. Cf. 1867a: 713)

15. For helpful surveys, see Geras (1985) and Lukes (1985).

16. It is not easy to infer Marx's own commitments about the idea of justice from his comments. His concern is to 'discover what we are meant to understand by the phrase "just distribution" *as used here*' (Marx, 1875: 344; emphasis added), and 'here' refers to the Gotha Programme itself, the document against which he fulminates.

17. It might be objected that on my own account in 4.2 Marx does define the proletariat quantitatively, in terms of how much of the means of production they own. But that definition relies on the threshold where quantitative difference carries qualitative significance, viz. owning so little that one has to enter into relations involving a large sacrifice of life.

18. For further discussion, see Graham (1990). I have concentrated on justice as a distributive notion. Reiman (1989) argues that Marx's critique requires the idea of *social* justice, based on an ideal of equal sovereignty. Justice in that sense comes much closer to the theory of interests I attribute to Marx.

/ f i v e /

Practice

In this chapter I discuss Marx's overriding, practical aim: the replacement of capitalism. He notoriously declined to write recipes for the cookshops of the future (Marx, 1873: 99) and has often been reproached for the sketchiness of his conception of an alternative society. I shall suggest that his views on the exceedingly stringent preconditions for realizing that society explain his sketchiness. I hope it will emerge how far Marx's views are from those of many Marxist movements and regimes.

Engels explains how he and Marx used the terms 'socialism' and 'communism' interchangeably at different times, depending on what they wished to distinguish their own position from, but always to express the idea of fundamental change in social relations and the need for the proletariat itself to carry out its own emancipation (Engels, 1888: 64–5). Over the last hundred years both terms have accumulated too many misleading associations for expressing those aspirations. I therefore use the more neutral term 'future society'.

5.1 The Future Society

In accordance with his general theory, Marx defined capitalism in material rather than superstructural (for example, political) terms (see 4.1). Commodities predominate, and the system is based on the worker's sale of labour-power as a commodity. We must make sense of Marx's projected alternative at the same level. Like capitalism, the organization of the future society is 'essentially economic' (Marx and Engels, 1932: 87). Marx therefore sponsors revolutions which 'really challenge bourgeois conditions of life, rather than affecting only its political formations' (Marx, 1850: 131). To that end, he reminds us of the historical specificity of our own epoch:

> ... nature does not produce on the one hand owners of money or commodities, and on the other hand men possessing nothing but their own labour-power. This relation has no basis in natural history, nor does it have a social basis common to all periods of human history. (Marx, 1867a: 273)

Retaining that sense of historical specificity is not easy. As an aid Marx provides examples where capitalist relations do not obtain: the payments and services in kind of feudalism; the labour in common of a patriarchal peasant family whose collective products do not confront them as commodities; and an 'association of free men, working with the means of production held in common' (*ibid.*: 171). We shall return to the last.

According to Marx's general theory, productive forces tend to develop through history, but this periodically necessitates fundamental changes in the relations of production through which they develop (3.4). His proposal for the future society conforms to this combination of continuity and discontinuity. The productive forces are to be retained and developed, but not in that form which implies the production relations peculiar to capitalism: not as commodities and capital.

We have seen that Marx celebrates the productive potential provided by capitalism, which could be used to lighten arduous toil, give human beings material security, and release them from the burden which prevents them from fulfilling other aspirations. One of the 'civilizing aspects of capital' is that capitalist exploitation occurs in conditions that favour 'the creation of elements for a new and higher formation than was the case under the earlier forms of slavery, serfdom, etc.' (Marx, 1894: 958; cf. 1939: 162; Marx and Engels, 1848: 72). It points to a time when 'compulsion and the monopolization of social development (with its material and intellectual advantages) by one section of society at the expense of another disappears', and 'creates the material means and the nucleus for relations that permit this surplus labour to be combined, in a higher form of society, with a greater reduction of the overall time devoted to material labour' (Marx, 1894: 958).

Accordingly, Marx urges the need 'to distinguish between machinery and its employment by capital' (Marx, 1867a: 554). In capitalism the criterion for its employment is whether it will maximize the return on investment: it is 'a means for producing surplus-value' (*ibid.*: 492). Since it would be used in the future society for its labour-saving virtues, the 'field of application for machinery would therefore be entirely different . . . from what it is in bourgeois society' (*ibid.*: 515 n33). *Co-operation* is also to be preserved and transcended. It takes a particular form in capitalism, being 'employed by capital for the more profitable exploitation of labour' (*ibid.*: 453). It therefore 'appears to be a specific form of the capitalist process of production', but in fact it is 'a necessary concomitant of all production on a large scale' (*ibid.*). Its advantages can then be retained in other circumstances.

So much for continuity of productive forces. But on Marx's view, the production relations of capitalism must be eradicated before all these advantages can be realized.

> For us the issue cannot be the alteration of private property but only its annihilation, not the smoothing over of class antagonisms but the abolition of classes, not the improvement of existing society but the foundation of a new one. (Marx and Engels, 1885: 110)

He advocates 'the abolition of wage labour, capital and their mutual relationship' (Marx, 1850: 70).[1] While workers remain in the wage relation they must do whatever they can to reduce as far as possible the surplus labour they give up. But he insists that this struggle is distinct from the more important enterprise of abolishing the conditions which necessitate it:

> Instead of the *conservative* motto, *A fair day's wage for a fair day's work!'* [the proletariat] ought to inscribe on their banner the *revolutionary* watchword, '*Abolition of the wages system!'* (Marx, 1898: 446; original emphasis)

Since money emerges from the exchange of commodities, and is itself a commodity playing a number of special roles (cf. 4.1), the abolition of commodities implies the abolition of money too, 'the abolition of buying and selling' (Marx and Engels, 1848: 82). Marx is therefore far from propounding any idea of 'market socialism'. He reminds us of the historical specificity of money. It existed before capital or wage labour, but often played 'little or no role within the individual communities, but only on their boundaries . . . By no means does it wade its way through all economic relations' (Marx, 1939: 103). He criticizes those, like Proudhon, who fail to see the connected nature of these different phenomena – exchange, money, wage labour and capital – and 'thereby reduce socialism to an elementary misunderstanding of the inevitable correlation existing between commodities and money' (Marx, 1859: 86; cf. 1867a: 188 n1, and 1939: 153–9).

In place of the capital–labour relation, 'capital is converted into common property, into the property of all members of society' (Marx and Engels, 1848: 81; cf. 1932: 84). Future society is 'the co-operative society based on common ownership of the means of production' (Marx, 1875: 345). Marx draws an analogy between a Robinson Crusoe and

> an association of free men, working with the means of production held in common, and expending their many different forms of labour-power in full self-awareness as one single social labour force. All the characteristics of Robinson's labour are repeated here, but with the difference that they are social instead of individual. All Robinson's products were exclusively the result of his own personal labour and they were therefore directly objects of utility for him personally. The total product of our imagined association is a social product. (Marx, 1867a: 171. More or less the same analogy occurs at Marx, 1939: 172–3)

The analogy emphasizes the collective nature of the future society, where property is 'no longer . . . private property . . . but rather . . . directly social property' (Marx, 1894: 568). The collective power developed in capitalism is redeployed so as to end the dominance of matter over people.

> . . . socialized man, the associated producers, govern the human metabolism with nature in a rational way, bringing it under their collective control instead of being dominated by it as a blind power; accomplishing it with the least expenditure of energy and in conditions most worthy and appropriate for their human nature. (ibid.: 959; cf. 1867a: 173)

This stress on collectivism may be thought to clash with perhaps the most famous passage in which Marx speaks of the future society. In capitalism individuals are confined to a particular role on pain of losing their livelihood, whereas in future society:

> where nobody has one exclusive sphere of activity but each can become accomplished in any branch he wishes, society regulates the general production and thus makes it possible for me to do one thing today and

another tomorrow, to hunt in the morning, fish in the afternoon, rear
cattle in the evening, criticize after dinner, just as I have a mind,
without ever becoming hunter, fisherman, shepherd or critic. (Marx and
Engels, 1932: 44–5; cf. Marx, 1867a: 618)

Whatever literal sense can be made of this metaphorical passage,
and although a concern with individuals is integral to Marx's
ontology (cf. 2.2), collective control, however, remains. This
freedom is available to individuals through *society's* regulating the
general production.

We should be cautious, nevertheless, in what we infer from the
stress on collectivism. In a modern complex society the com-
prehensive central planning of a command economy is sometimes
thought to be the only alternative to free market relations. Marx's
conception of the future society fits neither model. It implies that
control remains with the wider collective, rather than an elite or a
bureaucracy. (Such control is compatible with systems of delegation, provided that effective discretion to delegate remains with
the wider collective.) Of course, it will be objected that even if it
were possible to arrange a complex productive process in this way,
it would demand of members of the collective unprecedented
degrees of active involvement in social decisions and of social
responsibility in sticking to voluntary undertakings. Marx's
conception is indeed stringent in just that way. But that is a
different point, and it is important to see that for him the abolition
of commodity society does not entail the introduction of central
planning as that has normally been conceived.

Equally importantly, the introduction of central planning does
not entail the abolition of commodity society. The phrase *'free
market'* is not a pleonasm. It is perfectly possible to attempt to
regulate a system of commodity exchange by the mechanism of
centralized controls, and in various ways modern governments
attempt to do so. Regardless of their degree of success, if what is
being regulated is the exchange of *commodities* and a system of
wage labour, then that state of affairs is quite distinct from Marx's
proposed future society.

This is important in the light of purported empirical embodiments of Marx's principles. Socialism is often equated with
nationalization of the means of production (cf. Roemer, 1982a: 3,
Wright, 1985: 83–4), which may itself be thought to represent 'a
radical equalization of ownership of capital: everyone owns one
citizen-share' (Wright, *ibid*.). Cunningham suggests that a society
will be non-capitalist:

either if nobody privately owns means of production and employs workers or if the allocative discretion by those who do is severely constrained, not by the market but by social and political structures deliberately put in place to further goals other than to protect continuing capitalist discretion. (Cunningham, 1987: 82)

Further, 'a noncapitalist society, and in particular a socialist one, is compatible with there being a measure of capitalist ownership' (*ibid.*: 315 n3).

It is true that in the *Communist Manifesto* Marx talks of the need 'to centralize all instruments of production in the hands of the state' (Marx and Engels, 1848: 86). However, the state is here explicitly characterized as 'the proletariat organized as the ruling class' (*ibid.*); and the purpose of centralization is to increase productive forces as rapidly as possible, preparatory to a state of affairs where 'all production has been concentrated in the hands of a vast association of the whole nation' (*ibid.*: 87).[2] Hence for Marx the essential contrast is not between private and state ownership but between private and *common*, or collective, ownership. Whether the state owns capital or each citizen owns an equal share, if capital survives then so, on Marx's view, do the attendant circumstances of a society based on capital. If commodities, capital and wage labour are connected in the ways he believes, that explains why he advocates the abolition of all together. He will regard the aspiration to equal ownership of capital as vain, if concentration of capital is a prerequisite for a system of wage labour. He will acknowledge the possibility of placing constraints on capitalist discretion: his insistence on the need to resist capitalist encroachments while still in the capital-labour relation attests to that. But, given the symbiotic relation he perceives between capital and wage labour, and the unacceptability of the latter, any system in which capital remains will fail to match his conception of the future society.

Even if resources are collectively owned, individuals' needs must be met. Marx holds that principles of distribution depend on the kind of social organization and on the corresponding level of social development. He assumes – 'but only for the sake of a parallel with the production of commodities' (Marx, 1867a: 172) – that distribution is determined by labour-time contributed. In a similar way, in the *Critique of the Gotha Programme* he entertains[3] the idea that, at the outset of the future society, individuals might receive work-certificates indicating how much they could withdraw from the social wealth for consumption (Marx, 1875: 346).

Arguably, such a principle ignores Marx's own strictures and misses the point of the Crusoe analogy. Marx holds that if 'the material conditions of production were the co-operative property of the workers themselves a different distribution of the means of consumption from that of today would follow of its own accord' (*ibid.*: 348). It is dubiously consistent with this to say that when such co-operative circumstances obtain, 'the same principle [of distribution] is at work here as that which regulates the exchange of commodities as far as this is an exchange of equal values' (*ibid.*: 346). Moreover, already in capitalism measurement of individual contribution becomes problematic, because one portion of output is attributable to co-operative effort itself (Marx, 1867a: 447).

Doubts about the suggested principle of distribution go deeper. Exchange presupposes an owner and a non-owner of something. Crusoe cannot give himself, or exchange with himself, what he already owns. Similarly, if all own the means of production collectively, there are no non-owners of them and they cannot therefore be exchanged. Common ownership is distinct from *any* form of sectional ownership: it transcends particular dispositions of property and is in a sense a negation of ownership altogether. As Marx puts it: 'Within the co-operative society based on common ownership of the means of production the producers do not *exchange* their products' (Marx, 1875: 345; emphasis added). The future society 'deprives no man of the power to appropriate the products of society' (Marx and Engels, 1848: 82). If *we*, collectively, own productive resources, then *we*, collectively, have the power of disposal over them.

This argument is not entirely convincing. The future society involves collective ownership of *productive resources*, whereas we are now discussing the distribution of *products*, the fruits of those resources. Perhaps mines and systems of transportation can be collectively owned, and perhaps if there are no non-owners the concept of ownership ceases to have any application. But the same cannot be true of hats and toothbrushes and bowls of rice. These must eventually belong to designated people, if ownership is defined in terms of effective control. The question of distribution therefore remains.

Marx's reply would be that it is problematic only in the initial stages of the future society. When it is properly established and 'all the springs of wealth flow more abundantly', then distribution proceeds according to the principle 'From each according to his abilities, to each according to his needs' (Marx, 1875: 347). Indeed, abundance is a precondition for the future society:

... so long as the productive forces are still insufficiently developed to make competition superfluous, and therefore would give rise to competition over and over again, for so long the classes which are ruled would be wanting the impossible if they had the 'will' to abolish competition. (Marx and Engels, 1932: 358)

Marx's claims may be thought highly implausible, but we should not exaggerate them. Lukes, for example, describes the 'un-realizable state of affairs' of 'co-operative abundance' as 'eliminating non-compatible desires' (Lukes, 1985: 32). Cohen objects that abundance can never be so great 'that no one will be under the necessity of abandoning or revising what he wants, because of the wants of other people' (Cohen, 1990b: 38). Elster lists as one of the elements of Marx's thought 'the notion that social decision-making can occur without conflict, by unanimous approval or election' (Elster, 1985: 526).

No doubt these states of affairs are unrealizable, but Marx need not disagree. He is concerned with the rooted, irreconcilable conflicts of class interest in capitalist society: antagonisms 'not in the sense of individual antagonism but of an antagonism that emanates from the individuals' social conditions of existence' (Marx, 1859: 21). These are endemic conflicts of material interest of a particularly fundamental kind, and since he believes that the material mode of production conditions social, political and intellectual life, we may presume that he thinks their removal will help to remove other conflicts. But he has no need to embrace the extreme view that it will remove all conflicts of interest whatsoever, or produce a society where no one ever abandons what they want in the light of others' wants.[4]

On the contrary, with collective resources under collective control, it might be rational for individuals to do just that. I argued in 2.5 that in some circumstances one can justifiably regard the decisions of a collective to which one belongs as one's own, and therefore as something one should identify with. Collective practical identification of that kind may impose restrictions on the inclinations which one would follow if one were reasoning in some other capacity than that of a member of the collective itself. For Marx, the behaviour of an individual in the future society would exemplify this kind of identification.

Marx does believe that abundance, in some sense, is attainable. But, like many of his theses, this one requires refinement and qualification, and assessing its plausibility is more complex than might be thought, raising interconnected conceptual, normative and empirical questions. It may even be misleading to suggest that Marx postulates a situation where society can 'leave work unpaid and provide goods free of charge, without generating shortages' (Van Parijs, 1989: 475). Marx speaks of *needs*, not wants or preferences. The concept of need is elliptical, and for a complete thought we must specify what someone needs something *for*. At the limit are 'course-of-life' needs: those which must be met for living a reasonably normal, average life (cf. Braybrooke, 1987: 29–31). This is what Marx is concerned with: 'personal appropriation of the products of labour, an appropriation that is made for the maintenance and reproduction of human life' (Marx and Engels, 1848: 81). That echoes the elaborated definition of the working class in 4.2, covering those who must sell their labour-power in order to live such an average life. What the future society removes is 'the miserable character of this appropriation' (*ibid.*), the necessity of entering into the wage relation to that end, with all the consequences Marx claims to follow from living in a society based on that transaction.

It is a contentious matter what the scope of such ordinary needs is (cf. Geras, 1983: 72 ff., 83). They presumably include means of sustenance and exclude moon rockets, but that leaves room for debate about other elements. For example, some degree of medical care must be included, but how much, and of what degree of sophistication? There will also be problems about the level of abstraction at which needs are identified. People need adequate means of transportation, but do they need cars?

But will refinement and qualification save Marx's belief from its obvious falsity? Commentators standardly attack its utopian[5] nature. Nove asks rhetorically:

> But is it conceivable, can it be seriously envisaged, that the world's citizenry would be able to take whatever they wanted (even 'reasonably' wanted) from the amply supplied public stores . . .? Given that today most of the people of China and India, which together number over 1,500 million, live in dire poverty, have the 'limitless resources' optimists ever tried to calculate the resource implications of China's millions eating as much meat as, say, even the East Europeans do today? (Nove, 1983: 16–17)

Marx is entitled to ask us to engage in a difficult calculative exercise before pronouncing. In determining what resources are available for human needs in the future society, we cannot simply calculate what might be available in a capitalist society without the cash tills and checkouts. We must include resources diverted by capitalism from satisfying human need: not only those currently not used at all (for example, human skills and technology unused where there is no prospect of profit) but also those used solely for the purpose of sustaining some aspect of capitalist society (among which will be at least all costs of keeping private property private: a monetary system, banking, insurance arrangements and related activities).

The calculation is open-ended in other ways. Current practices regarding product innovation, or built-in obsolescence, fit in well with the demands of commodity society, but are they necessary otherwise? Is it necessary to have such a wide range of slightly differing consumer durables of a given type, updated frequently with resultant costs in terms of design, advertising, accounting, and the like? We should remember, too, not just immediate expenditure but also the massive use of human energies involved indirectly in these processes, as well as various kinds of ancillary workers. Similar questions might be raised about personal possession of large numbers of consumer durables on a household basis, most remaining unused for most of the time, or personal car ownership, as compared with an efficient, comfortable and reliable system of public transportation relying on already-available technology.

Further indeterminacy arises if some of Marx's more ambitious theses are correct. To take just one example: if modern wars are the consequence of capitalist rivalry for markets, spheres of influence, strategic control of territory, and so on, rather than innate aggressive tendencies in human nature which can find no other suitable outlet, then the vast resources used for that purpose would themselves be available for use of more direct value to human beings. Rhetorical questions about calculation of resources are therefore double-edged. It may be no easier to rule out Marx's abundance thesis than to rule it in.

Many difficult questions remain, such as what principles of distribution would govern preferences, as opposed to needs. But it might be said that, in any case, the real problem with the idea of taking according to need stems not from the question of available resources but from the question of what can reasonably be expected of human behaviour, and whether people themselves could have any basis for knowing how much to take. By concentrating on productive resources Marx 'side-steps the issue, by resorting to a technological fix' (Cohen, 1990b: 35).

Marx certainly does not believe that the technical availability of abundance resolves all these difficult problems of human interaction or choice of social priorities. Abundance is part of the specification of future society, but he recognizes that major changes must precede its inauguration. The working class:

> have no ready-made utopias. . . . They know that in order to work out their own emancipation . . . they will have to pass through long struggles, through a series of historical processes, transforming circumstances and men. (Marx, 1871: 213)

The appearance of abundance does not suddenly transform people; they gradually transform themselves and their circumstances in a way which makes abundance possible.

This suggestion is consistent with the dynamics governing the trajectory from one epoch to another in diachronic materialism. Material conditions decide 'whether or not the periodically recurring revolutionary convulsion will be strong enough to overthrow the basis of the entire existing system' (Marx and Engels, 1932: 50). But those conditions consist *both* of the state of productive forces *and* of 'the formation of a revolutionary mass, which revolts not only against separate conditions of society up till then, but against the very "production of life" till then, the "total activity" on which it was based' (*ibid.*: 50–51). If *both* conditions are not propitious, the revolution fails.

The distinctness of Marx's conception of the future society from any notion of state ownership or control of capital and commodities has implications for contemporary assessment of his theories. Roemer sees 'a crisis in Marxian theory, evidenced by its lack of success in explaining the behavior of and developments in modern socialist countries' (Roemer, 1982a: 2). Regimes claiming Marx's name displayed enormously embarrassing features: they departed entirely from democratic practices, contained elites in positions of great privilege and power over the majority of the populace, and remained economically unsuccessful. If Marxism cannot account for these failures, then both Marx's theory and his practical aspirations may be thought to be vain.

If these societies had met Marx's specification of the future society and in addition exhibited the embarrassing features, this objection would be well taken. But he is entitled to respond that they were no test of his views, since they failed to meet his specification in the first place. This rejoinder does not fall into the error, noted by Roemer, of 'concluding that the society in question cannot be socialist because it displays certain features which are bad' (*ibid.*: 5). On the contrary, such societies fail to measure up to Marx's conception because they are founded on wage labour and the exchange of goods on a market.

The same can be said in reply to Parkin's objection that the embarrassing features faced Marxists with

> the unwelcome choice of either having to expand the definition of capitalism to embrace socialist society, or of disowning the cherished concepts of private property and surplus extraction upon which their class theory is grounded. (Parkin, 1979: 24)

We have seen that Marx's definition of capitalism is already couched in terms of the predominance of objects produced for exchange, a system of wage labour and the existence of a minority in effective control of productive resources. To that extent, the appearance of familiar features in these societies, far from being an embarrassment for Marx's theory, actually constitutes a piece of confirmation for it (albeit of a relatively weak kind). They provide one more confirming instance for the general claim that if production is based on exchange, then these other features necessarily follow.

However, the objection can be reformulated. The creators of Marxist regimes were, surely, inspired by Marx's own ideas and set out to realize his aspirations? Does their manifest and complete failure not suggest that there is something suspect about those aspirations? Did not Marx's theories themselves sow the seeds of what followed?

These questions are reasonable, but all we have so far is an account of Marx's conception (such as it is) of the future society. He also has views about the circumstances in which that conception is realizable. It will become apparent in 5.2 that his account of the preconditions for establishing the future society itself helps to explain the failure of Marxism: it diverged widely at crucial points from Marx's own prescriptions.

One such precondition may be mentioned now. Marx observes that capitalist industry

> ... produced world history for the first time, insofar as it made all civilized nations and every individual member of them dependent for the satisfaction of their wants on the whole world. (Marx and Engels, 1932: 75–6; cf. 1848: 71, 85)

Consequently, the class struggle between proletariat and bourgeoisie is national in form but 'not in substance' (Marx and Engels,

1848: 78). Capitalism must be replaced on a worldwide level. 'Empirically, communism is only possible as the act of the dominant peoples "all at once" and simultaneously . . .' (Marx and Engels, 1932: 46–7; cf. 1848: 85; Marx, 1850: 45, 111–12).

Marx makes that point in connection with Russia, where primitive forms of common ownership of land survived. The question arose whether it could pass straight to the common ownership characteristic of the future society, or whether it would have to go through the same evolutionary process as the West.

> The only answer to that possible today is this: If the Russian Revolution becomes the signal for a proletarian revolution in the West, so that both complement each other, the present Russian common ownership of land may serve as the starting-point for a communist development. (Marx and Engels, 1882: 24; cf. 1932: 91)

The embarrassing societies in question, therefore, do not only fail to meet the basic specification laid down by Marx. He would have held that it was out of the question that the future society should be realized in one part of the world, while the rest of it remained locked in capitalist relations. That clearly raises to a wholly new level of stringency the requirements for the prospective transformation of society.

Why should Marxist movements have come to prevail which diverged widely from Marx, on this and (as we shall see) on many other matters? That is a massively complex historical question, and it may be foolhardy for a philosopher even to venture an opinion. But, as with many questions about the Marxist tradition, my preference is for explanations which the tradition itself would stigmatize as heretical. More marginal traditions have recognized the radical nature of Marx's conception of the future society and argued from an early stage that Russia, for example, did not represent a break with all forms of capitalism in the way or in the conditions that he required.[6]

This is argued by the Dutch anti-Bolshevik revolutionary Anton Pannekoek. By the start of the twentieth century the world was different in at least two respects from the world Marx had encountered: capitalism had become the dominant world system; and Marx's own theories were available. Capitalism was not entrenched in every part of the world. In particular Russia, with pockets of industry and heavily dependent on foreign capital, was largely a semi-feudal country with a vast downtrodden peasantry. It did not have a strong indigenous bourgeoisie, but it did have an intelligentsia which had learnt from Marx the general idea of historical development. Circumstances at this time are therefore very different in Western and Eastern Europe:

> Marxism in Western Europe is the world view of a working class confronting the task of converting a most highly developed capitalism ... into communism. The Russian workers and intellectuals could not make this their object; they had first to open the way for a free development of a modern industrial society. (Pannekoek, 1938: 96)

The heretical thought can then be advanced that the role (though not the intention) of the Russian Revolution is to entrench capitalism, the system of production based on commodities and the sale and purchase of labour-power, albeit in a vastly different form from that prevailing elsewhere. The state, rather than private individuals, becomes the capitalist. Hence:

> the Russian revolution is a bourgeois revolution, like the French one of 1789: at the economic level, its essential content has been the transformation of the peasantry into freeholders and small producers; at the political level, it represents the coming to power of a new bureaucracy. ... Of course, there are big differences between these two revolutions in regard to class relationships, degree of development, orientation of the movement and perspectives, which are not taken into account here. (Pannekoek, 1921; cited in Bricianer, 1978: 229)

How, then, does the adoption of Marx's theories fit into this scenario? Pannekoek argues that

> the alleged Marxism of Lenin and the bolshevist party is nothing but a legend. ... Marxism, however, at the same time shows the necessity of the legend; every middle-class revolution, requiring working-class and peasant support, needs the illusion that it is something different, larger, more universal. Here it was the illusion that the Russian revolution was the first step of world revolution liberating the entire proletarian class from capitalism ... (Pannekoek, 1938: 97–8)

This explanation is consistent with Marx's theories. Recall his distinction between the material transformation of a society and the ideological forms in which the protagonists fight out the changes, on analogy with an individual and their own opinion of themselves (3.1, 3.4). By the same token, a movement might see itself as carrying out Marx's programme when in fact it was doing something quite different. Recall, too, his suggestion that an ascendant class struggling to displace a ruling class does indeed need to represent its interests as more general (3.5). It will be especially difficult to meet that need when transformations of the type in question (the move to capitalism) have already taken place elsewhere *and* when a theoretical apparatus is available which has the power to discredit the new systems resulting from the transformation. In those circumstances, a particularly powerful ideology is called for as a motivating force impelling people to struggle for the change in places where it has not yet fully occurred. What more powerful ideology than that of Marxism itself, with its promise not of bringing in the new system whose disadvantages are becoming apparent, but of sweeping it away in favour of a newer system still? We can conclude, then, not merely that problematic 'socialist' societies do not fit Marx's specification of the future society and *do* fit his specification of the main essential features of capitalist society. Marx's own theories can explain why such historical developments might occur.[7]

5.2   The Route to the Future Society

Suppose that Marx has provided at least a skeletal conception of a desirable future society. What developments would have to occur, on his assumptions, for it to be realized? Commentators differ about the connection between Marx's practical proposals and his materialism. Roemer suggests that 'Marxism's revolutionary role is . . . a corollary of its theory of historical materialism' and it is 'conceivable that a modern historical materialist re-evaluation will decide that socialism is not possible' (Roemer, 1982a: 4). Cohen holds that 'scepticism about historical materialism should leave the socialist project more or less where it would otherwise be' (Cohen, 1988: 132). The

> political applicability of historical materialism is limited, since it is a theory about *epochal* development, and the time horizon of political action necessarily falls short of the epochal. (*ibid.*: 133 n2; original emphasis)

However, the content of Marx's conception of the future society implies that he wished people to widen their political horizons: not to content themselves with relatively minor changes in their conditions of life, but to initiate fundamental changes – epochal changes in a qualitative sense. Since that commitment to fundamental change is dominant, Marx is also committed to urging adoption of long-term goals if necessary, and that may affect the kind of political movement to which his ideas lead.

There is clearly a link between Marx's politics and his *basic* materialism. Material circumstances are central in any account of human interests, and the theory of exploitation in capitalism is meant to show where the fundamental interests of the working class lie. The connection with the materialism of his general theory is more complex. He believes that the prospective transformation to the future society conforms in *certain* respects to the pattern of earlier transitions, but also has unique features.

Recall the dynamics of epochal change in diachronic materialism. Productive forces tend to increase until the existing relations of production begin to fetter their development. The relations then change, as a result of revolutionary upheaval. These transformations occur when propitious material circumstances and the actions of classes converge. Recall, too, the distinction between the material transformation and the ideological forms in which human agents become conscious of the conflict and fight it out. Collective human action is required to fuel the trajectory from one social system into another, and the protagonists must have *some* conception of what they are doing. But it may be inaccurate, and this may itself be functional for the change in question. A subordinate class may support a class in the ascendant, in the mistaken perception that general liberation is in prospect.

For Marx the prospective transformation conforms to the general pattern in requiring a similar convergence of material circumstances and human efforts. Earlier attempts by the proletariat failed, 'owing to the then undeveloped state of the proletariat, as well as to the absence of the economic conditions for its emancipation' (Marx and Engels, 1848: 94). The 'material and mental conditions of the negation of wage labour and of capital' must await the point at which wage labour 'is necessarily stripped off as a fetter' (Marx, 1939: 749).

However, the prospective transformation also has unique features. We saw how, on Marx's general view, new classes were able to enlist the support of a broad mass in their fight to gain ascendancy over and replace an old exploiting class. New relations of exploitation then came into existence:

All the preceding classes that got the upper hand, sought to fortify their already acquired status by subjecting society at large to their conditions of appropriation. (Marx and Engels, 1848: 78; cf. 1932: 83)

This pattern is broken with the proletariat, who 'have nothing of their own to secure and fortify' (Marx and Engels, 1848: 78), no characteristic form of wealth appropriation to consolidate, in some new set of social relations of production. Hence their defeat of the capitalist class will entail the end of wealth appropriation, and therefore of exploitation, altogether.

Accordingly, the prospective transformation involves not merely the replacement of one set of property relations with another but the abolition of sectional ownership of means of production, the abolition of class society altogether. The 'last form of servitude assumed by human activity, that of wage labour on one side, capital on the other, is thereby cast off like a skin' (Marx, 1939: 749). The proletarian revolution 'abolishes the rule of all classes with the classes themselves' (Marx and Engels, 1932: 85).

The uniqueness of the prospective transformation carries vital implications for the route to be followed for its achievement. Marx says:

> All previous historical movements were movements of minorities, or in the interest of minorities. The proletarian movement is the *self-conscious*, *independent* movement of the immense *majority*, in the interest of the immense majority. (Marx and Engels, 1848: 78; emphasis added)

These three aspects of the route to the future society – *self-consciousness*, *independence* and *majoritarianism* – need further examination.

Whereas any movement to change social relations must have *some* consciousness, the more stringent requirement that the proletariat be *self*-conscious implies an absence of misperception. Since there is no other class to subjugate, general liberation *is* in prospect and the proletarian movement need not represent its struggle, either to itself or to others, as anything other than what it really is. The prospective transformation, unlike earlier ones, is *transparent*: carried out by people who are clearly aware of what they are doing and what their role is. To echo Marx's analogy, the proletarian movement is like the individual whose opinion of themselves *can* be relied upon.

This self-consciousness is not just an optional increase in social understanding. It follows from the nature of the future society, as outlined in 5.1, that it must be sustained by people clearly aware of what they are doing, actively and voluntarily co-operating in arranging social production. It is literally unthinkable that a population should organize its affairs according to such principles without being aware that this is what they were doing. People can be coerced or duped into doing what they themselves do not comprehend or desire, but they cannot be coerced or duped into doing what they voluntarily choose to do.

True, it is not in the same way unthinkable that people might carry out the changes which *result* in that society, though unaware at the time of what they are engaged in. But at what point is an unclouded perception acquired? It would be akin to a belief in magic to suppose that this suddenly happens at the point where they actually find themselves participating in the new relations requiring perspicacious understanding. The only remaining plausible alternative is that such understanding is acquired *in the course of* this movement for fundamental social change, change effected by a class 'from which emanates the consciousness of the necessity of a fundamental revolution' (Marx and Engels, 1932: 85). As Marx puts it: 'for the success of the cause itself, the alteration of men on a mass scale is necessary' (*ibid.*: 86). The proletariat has numbers on its side, but 'numbers weigh only in the balance, if united by combination and led by knowledge' (Marx, 1864: 81). This insistence on a massive change in consciousness before the inception of the future society is the first indication of the gap between Marx and the vanguard Marxist tradition which sponsored a shorter and rougher route (cf. Graham, 1986a: 170–230).

According to Miliband, the appropriate consciousness consists solely in an understanding of the need to overthrow capitalism and the will to do so (Miliband, 1977: 33). In the light of the history of political movements claiming Marx's name, he (rightly) wishes to dissociate Marx from the idea that 'true' class consciousness demands subscription to some particular precept, strategy or organization. That turns class consciousness into 'a catechismal orthodoxy, departure and dissent from which become grave – and punishable – offences' (*ibid.*: 35). By contrast, Marx points out that the rules of the First International leave 'the details of theory to be worked out as inspired by the demands of the practical struggle, and as growing out of the exchange of ideas among the sections, with an equal hearing given to all socialist views in their journals and congresses' (Marx and Engels, 1872a: 299). The limit to flexibility is that sections are understood to be 'all seeking the same object, and all accepting the same programme – a programme

limited to outlining the major features of the proletarian movement' (*ibid.*).

However, making revolutionary consciousness depend on mere
assent to the overthrow of capitalism is both imprecise and
incomplete. It is imprecise because there is more than one
conception of capitalist society (cf. 4.1). Unity around the slogan to
overthrow capitalism could therefore mask fundamentally different conceptions of the thing to be overthrown. Marx is explicit
on that point, and it is apposite that proletarian consciousness
should be so too. It must involve a determination specifically to
abolish all forms of society dominated by commodities and by the
wage-relation on which their production depends. Such a determination leaves ample room for debate about the precise form
abolition is to take, but it already places a very clear and strong
demand on proletarian consciousness. A determination to overthrow capitalism *in Marx's sense*, to be rid of all forms of the
commodity-dominated society, is a phenomenon much less
frequently encountered than a dissatisfaction with this or that
particular aspect of some particular form of commodity society.

The incompleteness of the formulation in terms of a determination to overthrow capitalism arises from the fact that such
overthrow does not necessarily amount to arrival in the future
society. It might herald chaos, complete social dislocation. The
will to overthrow must therefore be supplemented by a will and a
capacity to replace capitalism with the relations outlined in 5.1.
Marx says:

> Communism is for us not a *state of affairs* which is to be established, an
> *ideal* to which reality [will] have to adjust itself. We call communism
> the *real* movement which abolishes the present state of things. (Marx
> and Engels, 1932: 47; original emphasis)

This explains his reluctance to be drawn on the nature of the
institutions of the future society (5.1), and places responsibility for
specifying them squarely on the proletariat. The future society is
in a certain way self-defining. Its population voluntarily co-operate
to create the society they wish to have. That requires the
proletariat itself to form clear and practical views on the
procedures and practices which it prefers and which are necessary
for the future society to function. It must be prepared to take a
very much less passive role in social life than at present, not only
in the future society but before its inception. If the proletariat does
not write recipes for the cookshops, there is no feast.

Design of the institutions for a new society is a daunting task, and it indicates in yet a further way the stringency of the requirements of the transformation. But it is at least not as absurd to make these demands of the proletariat as it is of an individual theorist. Collectives often have massive powers in ways not available to individuals (cf. 2.4). If Marx is correct, the proletariat already functions as an unconscious collective, with multiple talents and skills (4.3). Those talents and skills remain available if it begins to function as a conscious collective, with a revolutionary set of aims. No less would be required for the construction of a new society, but no less would be available. Nor is this task to be accomplished from scratch. The present state of things, the production relations of capitalism, is abolished, but the whole society is not obliterated. Just as productive forces are retained, so many institutions may be adapted to different objectives. The proletariat does not have to devise means of communication, transportation, decision-making, and so on, *ab initio*. However, if consciousness in this form is a prerequisite for the transformation, then revolutionary class consciousness is again far rarer than it has generally been taken to be.

The proletarian movement is also, according to Marx, *independent*. His standing conviction is that the proletariat itself must replace current relations of production with new ones. Revolutionary consciousness may arise among other classes 'through the contemplation of the situation of this class' (Marx and Engels, 1932: 85; cf. 1848: 77), but his emphasis is consistently on the importance of self-emancipation. He drafted that notion into the Provisional Rules of the First International (Marx, 1864: 82), and later insisted that 'collective appropriation can only proceed from a revolutionary action of the class of producers – the proletariat – organized in an independent political party' (Marx, 1880: 376; cf. Engels, 1888: 63).

There are two aspects here. On the one hand, no agency, distinct from the proletariat, can provide its emancipation from without. Marx rejects any notion of class philanthropy in a letter to the leaders of the German Social-Democratic Workers' Party:

When the International was formed, we expressly formulated the battle-cry: the emancipation of the working class must be the work of the working class itself. We cannot ally ourselves, therefore, with people who openly declare that the workers are too uneducated to free themselves and must first be liberated from above by philanthropic big bourgeois and petty bourgeois. (Marx and Engels, 1879: 375)

This accords with his dissociation from common moral assumptions (cf. 4.4) and his preference for collective interest and collective identification, rather than altruism, as bases for social action (cf. 2.5, 3.5, 3.6).

On the other hand, the proletariat cannot expect any agency from within to relieve it of the burden of emancipating itself. The future society depends on voluntary association, not economic compulsion or coercion. It therefore demands a high level of self-motivated and responsible behaviour on the part of its inhabitants, rather than passive dependence on the direction of others. As with the required self-consciousness, these qualities must be present in the future society itself and are most plausibly acquired in the course of the movement which eventually creates it. Self-emancipation implies the need for the class itself, rather than some active minority, to take part in fundamental social change. It places some restriction on passive dependence on leadership – on some interpretations of leadership at least.

Miliband argues that any model of the revolutionary process must include a structure of command, given the heterogeneity of the working class and the 'permanent and intractable divisions which exist in this as in any other social aggregate' (Miliband, 1977: 123–7). The condition of different members of the proletariat varies enormously, and this does create conflicting interests in many circumstances, but it is not a compelling reason for the inevitability of a structure of command. Marx distinguishes the early, sectarian phase of proletarian struggle, when 'the proletariat has not yet reached the stage of being sufficiently developed to *act as a class*' (Marx and Engels, 1872a: 298; emphasis added). By contrast, in the International proletarians are 'linked together in common struggle' and its rules 'only speak of *workers'* societies, all seeking the same object and all accepting the same programme' (*ibid.*: 299; original emphasis). Workers must unite *as* workers, taking as a political priority their common interest in escaping from the condition which they share, rather than focusing on the characteristics which divide them and set their interests against one another. That implies unity on fundamentals, though not necessarily uniformity. There might, for example, be divergent views on how the movement should progress. But that does not yet dictate a structure of command: only an authoritative means of resolving disagreements.

No doubt some forms of interaction which might be called leadership are indispensable for effective political action. For example, Elster says: 'Obviously, leaders are always necessary, regardless of the motivation of individuals, to co-ordinate collective action' (Elster, 1985: 366; cf. Levine, Sober and Wright, 1987: 81–2). The requirements of co-ordination do imply a distinctive role for co-ordinators, but not necessarily a superior position of power. Marx employs the analogy of a conductor of an orchestra to make the point that direction and superintendence may be necessary, for example in the production process itself (cf. Marx 1867a: 448–9; 1894: 507, 510–11). But retention of that role may depend on the toleration of those under direction, so in that sense ultimate control remains with them. There is an indeterminately large range of possible relations between leaders and a wider body, with vastly differing degrees of control exercised by the wider body itself. Some will be compatible with the mooted independence of the proletarian movement; some will not. For example, various forms of delegation, or general instruction, or permission to direct under licence, on the conductor analogy, are compatible: ultimate power is not relinquished by the wider body. But a dependence on some sub-groups to provide the will and understanding for overcoming the production relations of capitalism, rather than this being present amongst the proletariat generally, would be incompatible with that independence.

There is a marked contrast here between Marx's insistence on independence and Lenin's famous views that the workers were incapable of reaching revolutionary consciousness by their own efforts, that it would have to be brought to them from without (Lenin 1902: 31–2, 78–9), and that a vanguard should seize power, although it could expect adequate support from the broad mass only *during or after* such seizure (Lenin, 1918: 32, 36). This assigns a far more passive role to the proletariat itself than Marx does.[8] But it may equally be doubted whether political parties as currently conceived could be adequate vehicles for the movement Marx sponsors, given his stringent requirements and his comment that *the whole class* must organize itself as a party. Cunningham speaks of the importance of 'trying to find organizational alternatives to traditional revolutionary vanguardism and to traditional social-democratic or labour politics' (Cunningham, 1987: 9). Marx would have agreed.

Marx holds that the movement consists of the immense *majority* of workers – unlike Lenin, who requires only 'a majority of the class-conscious, thinking and politically active workers' (Lenin, 1920: 69). He contrasts the transformation which brought about capitalist private property with the transformation which will end it:

In the former case, it was a matter of the expropriation of the mass of the people by a few usurpers; but in this case, we have the expropriation of a few usurpers by the mass of the people. (Marx, 1867a: 930)

Marx's conception of the working class thus has important political repercussions. If it is identified with those engaged in manual labour, it constitutes a small and probably shrinking proportion of the population. And, as Przeworski puts it, 'A party representing a class which has fewer members than the other classes combined cannot win electoral battles' (Przeworski, 1985: 24). This identification would therefore militate against acceptance of democratic political structures. On the other hand, identification of the working class by reference to dependence on sale of labour-power suggests a much wider band of the population, probably a majority. If you believe that the proletariat is in the process of becoming the majority class in society, and if you believe that this class is the only practical agency which can be expected to carry out and consolidate the desired transformation to the future society, then you have strong grounds for favouring democratic values. Universal suffrage and majority rule will be congenial institutions in that regard.

Marx says:

> The first step in the revolution by the working class is to raise the proletariat to the position of ruling class, to win the battle of democracy. (Marx and Engels, 1848: 86)

The legitimacy those institutions confer is of potential help for revolutionary purposes, since 'democratic conditions . . . endanger the very basis of bourgeois society' (Marx, 1850: 71).

> If the parliamentary regime lives by discussion, how can it forbid discussion? . . . How can any interest or institution then assert itself to be above thought, and impose itself as an article of faith? (Marx, 1852b: 190)

Marx also supports Chartism. Universal suffrage is 'the equivalent for political power for the working class of England, where the proletariat forms the large majority of the population'; it 'would be a far more socialistic measure than anything which has been honoured with that name on the Continent' (Marx, 1852a: 264). No doubt his enthusiasm is conditioned partly by his optimism that the English proletariat has already 'gained a clear consciousness of its position as a class' (*ibid.*). But much later he again refers to the possibility of universal suffrage being used for collective appropriation and thus being 'transformed from the instrument of fraud that it has been up till now into an instrument of emancipation' (Marx, 1880: 377). And he explicitly links the possibility of a non-violent transformation to 'victory through the polls' (Evans, 1975: 137).

Commitment to democratic values is distinct from commitment to narrowly *parliamentary* institutions.[9] Both Marx's synchronic materialism and his views on proletarian self-emancipation lead him to favour the supersession of those institutions. He says (and repeats): 'The working class cannot simply lay hold of the ready-made state machine, and wield it for its own purposes' (Marx, 1871: 206; cf. Marx and Engels, 1872b: 22; Engels, 1888: 66). That is what one would expect if the machine is part of a stabilizing superstructure for production relations which the proletariat must eradicate. If the working class must prepare itself for new relations, in which its own role is very much less passive, it will also need different and more appropriate institutions.

> The parliamentary regime leaves everything to the decision of majorities, why then should the great majority outside parliament not want to make the decisions? (Marx, 1852b: 190)

The endorsement of alternative democratic institutions is apparent in Marx's approving account of the Paris Commune, which stresses not just universal suffrage but the decentralized nature of the Commune's structure and the degree of control over delegates exercised by the wider citizen body (cf. Graham 1986a: 182–3).

> Instead of deciding once in three or six years which member of the ruling class was to misrepresent the people in parliament, universal suffrage was to serve the people, constituted in communes, as individual suffrage serves every other employer in the search for the workmen and managers in his business. (Marx, 1871: 210)

In both contexts, mistakes can be rectified as long as control is retained over those selected. And 'nothing could be more foreign to the spirit of the Commune than to supersede universal suffrage by hierarchic investiture' (*ibid.*: 211).

We should understand Marx's idea of the *dictatorship of the proletariat*, the form taken by the state during the period of revolutionary transformation, in the light of his approval of such arrangements. Nowhere does Marx state explicitly what form this dictatorship must take. Engels suggested that in order to find out we should look at the Paris Commune (Engels, 1891: 485) – a reasonable suggestion, since Marx describes the Commune as providing 'the political form ... under which to work out the economical emancipation of labour' (Marx, 1871: 212). It is sounder to work back from an account of the political arrangements which Marx favoured to a conclusion about what he must have had in mind when speaking of the dictatorship of the proletariat, rather than investing the phrase with an interpretation plainly at odds with the political forms he favoured. It then becomes clear that dictatorship here has nothing in common with the political forms so described in the twentieth century: it does not connote any kind of tyranny, and it is not counterposed to democracy (cf. Draper, 1986, 1987). It simply connotes temporary rule by the proletariat – the form the transition must take if it is indeed the self-conscious, independent movement of the immense majority. It is equally remote from the idea of the dictatorship of the proletariat in its historically most influential, Leninist, version, which diverges from Marx over the question of the proletariat's capacity to emancipate itself, and connectedly over the commitment to democratic values such as suffrage and majoritarianism (cf. Graham, 1986a: 212–15). That would more properly be called the dictatorship of the vanguard or the Party, and it has little licence in anything Marx himself thought.

It is very easy, of course, to parody this interpretation of Marx's thought. We are accustomed to the received picture of the amoral monster who gave rise to brutal forms of society in his own image, of how Marx inevitably paved the way for Stalin. We are now presented with the picture of the starry-eyed dreamer according to whom the world works in a remarkable and charming way. The working population cease to accord priority to watching television and tending the garden, and acquire revolutionary aspirations. They do so in an orderly and restrained manner, and create political structures without drastically unequal influence as between individuals. When the time is ripe, elections are called. The working population turn out to have won; and the ruling class, being democratic good sports, agree that they themselves have lost and give in gracefully. All this seems – to put it gently – an unlikely occurrence.

It may be objected that even if the development of such a movement were a serious possibility, it would be 'a *scale error* of monumental size and importance' to suppose that self-rule of a society can be assimilated to that of an individual (Elster, 1985: 458). Most especially in revolutionary circumstances, a strong state would be necessary to deal with 'the hostility and opposition of the new regime's internal and external enemies' (Miliband, 1977: 181). Internal enemies may be supposed among many higher and lower state officials (*ibid.*: 184), and we can assume that 'the political allegiance of . . . white-collar groups would be less than whole-hearted' (Parkin, 1979: 178). External enemies are likely in the form of 'powerful capitalist governments and international capitalist interests' (Miliband, 1977: 185).

Marx might reply that past precedents are not conclusive here: he has pointed to several crucial differences between the prospective transformation and earlier ones. It is apparent by now that if the prospective transformation is to occur, then the future must be in a number of respects dramatically different from the past; but if it were simply a matter of prediction based on inductive evidence, the case against Marx would be overwhelming. However, I suggest that Marx's point is best construed not as a prediction but as a *specification*. He certainly believes the transformation will occur, but his point here is to establish what conditions must be met *if* it is to occur. He asserts that the nature of the future society itself requires for its creation relatively auspicious circumstances, in certain explicitly and specifically stated respects, however unlikely it may be that they can obtain. Otherwise, it is simply ruled out until they prevail. This is distinct from saying whether or how that point can be reached.

This specification then carries implications for the question of opposition. If the transformation requires the active participation of the majority, then at least opposition must necessarily be less than active support. A balance in favour of opposition would simply render the revolutionary project inoperable. Whatever level of opposition does occur, Marx does not expect that the rulers will necessarily submit meekly, or out of democratic principle, to the wishes of the majority. He is committed to the idea that *force* may be necessary for the prospective transformation (e.g. Marx and Engels, 1848: 98). The specification, combined with this commitment, makes it plain that violence is not, on Marx's view, a primary instrument of the transformation. *Counter*-violence may be necessary in the event of resistance to the wishes of a clear majority, and it would be foolhardy not to budget for that possibility; but that is a different matter. Arguably, moreover, Marx is merely envisaging force where it would be legitimate even in conventional constitutional terms – namely, where there is resistance to the democratically expressed will of the majority. His main objective, however, is the growth in political consciousness and a connected growth in new forms of political organization, this side of the transformation, which would themselves create a new situation for fighting out class opposition.

That objective exonerates Marx from a common criticism. It is often held that Marxism 'has been unable to offer . . . an adequate response to injustice, violations of rights, and the resort to impermissible means, in the world we must live in' (Lukes, 1985: 141). As Miller puts it, 'a preference for socialism [does] not determine the choice among political means to that goal' (Miller, 1984: 63). Such views may seem to be reinforced if Marx is distanced from moral assumptions in the way I suggested in 4.4; but I have suggested in this section that even the most basic description of the future society provides an alternative source of restraint, and does determine (and preclude) certain means to that goal.

Marxism differed from Marx on the question of means and ends. Vanguardists were prepared to sacrifice present for future generations and operate through hugely authoritarian institutions, in the belief that those at present disabled from seeing where their interests lay would reach true consciousness in the future (cf. Graham, 1986a: 226–7). Marx rejects that paternalistic and necessarily speculative position. The future society must be reached by members of a class who, en route, become fitted to establish and sustain it. The minimal evidence for the possibility of a society of agents collectively controlling their own conditions of existence would be a mass political movement which did the same. Without the fulfilment of that condition, the future society is simply not an option.

Marx's view, in requiring evidence now rather than in the future, is both more appealing and less dangerous than vanguardism. Marx cannot demonstrate that he has not made a scale error in urging people to make collective decisions in the absence of authoritarian structures, in a manner analogous to individuals. Only a movement itself could do that (if anything could). If it failed, that would not begin to compare with the damage resulting from minorities making premature assaults on social institutions, in the name of a majority which did not share their views.

5.3 Revolutionary Motivation

I have spoken of the prospective transformation, but what *are* the prospects? Even if Marx has given a compelling account of the route which would have to be followed for the future society to be realized, that gives no reason to think it will be (cf. Elster, 1985: 75–6). Such reason may be thought to be provided by a particular scenario which can be drawn from Marx's writings. The revolutionary agency is constituted by the wretched of the earth, abject and downtrodden factory workers motivated by desperation. Their stake in the existing society is so minimal, they live in such desperate poverty, that even the dangers of social chaos are preferable. They have, after all, nothing to lose but their chains. Accordingly, it is only a matter of time before they act.

This scenario invites two general criticisms. First, though we might expect *revolt* from people in such straitened circumstances, how could we expect them to be capable, from their deprived and demoralized state, of reconstructing society along any more acceptable lines? (That thought may inspire disastrous vanguard theories.) Secondly, is this scenario not out of date? Nineteenth-century poverty has been alleviated (at least locally); most working people live a very different kind of life, and do have something to lose by embarking on revolution. There is no longer an agency of the proposed revolution fitting Marx's description.

Two recent commentators endorse the second criticism. Cohen describes how the

> communist impression of the working class was that its members
> 1. constituted the majority of society
> 2. produced the wealth of society
> 3. were the exploited people in society, and
> 4. were the needy people in society. (Cohen, 1990a: 374–5)

He then describes the political movements arising in response to the 'disintegration of the characteristics' listed: rainbow coalitions and needs-centred welfare-rights activism, for example (*ibid.*: 377–9).

Przeworski argues:

> In 1848 one simply knew who were the proletarians. One knew because all the criteria – the relation to the means of production, manual character of labor, productive employment, poverty, and degradation – all coincided to provide a consistent image ... in the middle of the nineteenth century the theoretical connotation of the concept of

proletariat, defined in terms of separation from the means of production, corresponded closely to the intuitive concept of proletariat conceived in terms of manual, principally industrial, laborers. (Przeworski, 1985: 56–7)

One century later, these criteria have come apart. People like lawyers and teachers fit the theoretical definition, but they 'neither act like proletarians nor think like proletarians' (*ibid.*: 57).

What are we to make of this? My suggestion is that when intuitive and theoretical concepts fall apart, Marx's stronger commitment is to the theoretical concept. He builds a theory of interests around the structural characteristic of separation from the means of wealth production, and the implications this has for human lives. In *Capital* that theory *precedes* the concrete descriptions of people's working conditions, which constitute an illustration of the deeper theoretical claim. But the theory itself must stand or fall independently of the particular circumstances of any particular group of people who possess that characteristic.

On the structural interpretation of Marx's thought developed in earlier chapters, it is not at all obvious that Cohen's four characteristics have fallen apart. People who belong to the working class on the definition elaborated in 4.2 probably do constitute the majority of society. They do produce the wealth of capitalist society in the form of theoretical interest to Marx – namely, that of contributing in multifarious ways to the production of surplus-value. They are exploited in the technical sense elaborated in 4.4: they belong to the collective which is as such responsible for the production of the whole surplus-value of society. Or – to speak more cautiously – if these claims are false, their falsity will depend on flaws in Marx's theory, rather than on contingent changes between nineteenth- and twentieth-century conditions.

Cohen's fourth characteristic is more problematic. Clearly, in terms of absolute levels of deprivation, there has been a massive change for many members of the working class between the two centuries. However, I indicated in 4.2 the evidence that for Marx the neediness of the proletariat is relative, both to the wealth of the capitalist class as defined in his theory and to society's state of development (cf. Marx, 1849: 94). Since our desires arise from society, 'we measure them, therefore, by society and not by the objects which serve for their satisfaction' (*ibid.*). If so, it is again less obvious that very visible changes in levels of material provision affect the claimed fourth characteristic.

Moreover, the historically current instantiation of Marx's

structural characterization, the whole group of people who are in the specified way separated from the means of life, is composed of such a wide collection of diverse talents that it is much less implausible to imagine this collective entity building a new society. It is not composed exclusively of abject wretches for whom that task might indeed be out of the question.

This way of defending Marx against the first general criticism may be thought to expose him very obviously to the second. The nineteenth-century wretches had plenty of reason for transforming society but little capacity; their twentieth-century replacements have plenty of capacity but little reason. Przeworski's point about lawyers and teachers can suggest more than just that they are strikingly unlike nineteenth-century manual workers. The transformation of society is surely a dangerous and risky business? Why should large numbers of people embark on it who find their conditions of existence perfectly tolerable, who are content to accept a trade-off involving the forfeit of a large quantity of waking hours for a given, rationed access to resources? Why should they *care* about relative wealth if their own access to real wealth is increasing? Even the abject can be expected to take such drastic steps only when conditions become so intolerable that they stand to lose less by doing so than not. (No doubt that is why much Marxist tradition expects revolution in conditions of crisis.) Those who are not abject will stand to lose far more. Why, then, should we imagine this broad band of heterogeneous people combining effectively together to turn the world upside down?

At his most optimistic, Marx holds that the process is 'inevitable', the bourgeoisie 'produces . . . its own grave-diggers' (Marx and Engels, 1848: 79). The natural laws of capitalism work 'with iron necessity' (Marx, 1867a: 91). The proletariat:

> becomes concentrated in greater masses, its strength grows, and it feels that strength more. The various interests and conditions of life within the ranks of the proletariat are more and more equalized, in proportion as machinery obliterates all distinctions of labour . . . (Marx and Engels, 1848: 75)

As capital is centralized, the need for co-operative labour grows, as does

> the revolt of the working class, a class constantly increasing in numbers, and trained, united and organized by the very mechanism of the capitalist process of production. (Marx, 1867a: 929; cf. *ibid.*: 635)

Moreover, while the proletariat gains new recruits, escape from it is possible only for those 'favoured by an exceptional fortune' (Marx, 1933: 1079). Generally, the proletarian 'has no chance of arriving at the conditions which would place him in the other class' (Marx and Engels, 1932: 94).

Marx's optimism about the inevitability of the transformation rests on at least four claims here: growth in the size of the proletariat; absence of class mobility; subjection of its members to increasingly similar conditions; and the fostering of increasing co-operation and co-ordination among the proletariat. On the interpretation of class proposed in 4.2, the first two claims are plausible. Whereas the proportion of people working at manual tasks in factories may not have grown, the proportion of those obliged to sell their labour-power probably has. And whereas there is no doubt a great deal of mobility *within* that broad class, escape *from* it, into the class of those who are under no compulsion to sell their labour-power, is probably comparatively rare. The third claim looks extremely implausible and, as I indicated in 4.3, contradicts Marx's recognition elsewhere that capitalism calls forth a hierarchy of labour-powers, with diverse conditions of life and levels of material provision among different members of the proletariat (cf. Marx, 1867a: 469). Let us suppose that the fourth claim is plausible – that the international nature of capitalism has produced ever greater co-operation on a worldwide scale.

The first, second and fourth claims combined give very weak support for Marx's optimism. All that follows is that a large and relatively stable collection of individuals combine in important ways into collectives in the productive process. Whereas that may generate powers without which the future society would not be possible, the collectives in question may be entirely unconscious (cf. 2.4). Their constituents may have no appreciation of the significance of their contribution to corporate activities. Given the very strong condition of self-consciousness which Marx placed on the agency of the transformation (5.2), there is nothing here to indicate why they must inevitably combine for that very different purpose. Lack of class mobility, for example, as construed here, gives no grounds. People may tend to make comparisons *within* the broad band of the working class, and then the comparative rarity of escape may count for very little in their consciousness.

Przeworski expresses a similar point:

The immediate experience of social relations, the experience based on income, the character of the work, the place in the market, the prestige of occupations, and so on, does not of itself become transformed into collective identification since this experience is mediated by the ideological and political practices of the movements engaged in the process of class formation. (Przeworski, 1985: 90)

Now at times Marx himself stresses the obstacles to the prospective transformation in ways which suggest a withdrawal from the strong claim that it is inevitable. If capitalism is said to aid the process of unifying the workers, it is also held responsible for dividing them:

> Competition separates individuals from one another, not only the bourgeois but still more the workers, in spite of the fact that it brings them together. (Marx and Engels, 1932: 77n)

This isolation can be overcome only after long struggles. Class conflict is like a war between two armies:

> each of which again carries on a battle within its own ranks, among its own troops. The army whose troops beat each other up the least gains the victory over the opposing host. (Marx, 1849: 84)

There are, therefore, counter-influences against that process of unification and collective identification which are prerequisites of the self-conscious movement needed to carry out the transformation. They include the perceived naturalness of capitalism:

> The advance of capitalist production develops a working class which by education, tradition and habit looks upon the requirements of that mode of production as self-evident natural laws. (Marx, 1867a: 899)

Marx distinguished his own politics from other traditions by the claim that historical circumstances now made the future society of 5.1 a peculiarly appropriate objective. The history of communism showed that it was immaterial whether the *idea* had been expressed a hundred times, if the productive forces and the revolutionary mass were not in place for its establishment (cf. Marx and Engels, 1932: 51). But now they were, having been produced by capitalism itself. The casting off of wage labour:

> is the result of the mode of production corresponding to capital; the material and mental conditions of the negation of wage labour and of capital . . . are themselves results of its production process. (Marx, 1939: 749)

If now he withdraws from the claim that the transformation from capitalism to the future society is inevitable, he must at least explain why the nature of capitalism itself makes it probable.[10]

Can he call on any resources from his general theory at this point? In his diachronic materialism he posited a dynamic according to which the transition from one epoch to another occurs when the relations of production cease to be propitious for the productive forces and begin to fetter them (3.4). We noted some of the ambiguities in the metaphor of fettering. It might occur *absolutely* or *relative* to some alternative social arrangements; and the *development* or the *use* of productive forces might become fettered. In 3.6 I suggested an interpretation of Marx's thesis about the development of productive forces. The suggestion was that if technological developments occur which are not taken up by the ruling group but are of potential benefit to non-ruling groups, then a coalition of such groups might combine in a struggle against the ruling group, wrest power away from them, and institute whatever new social relations were necessary for the use of the new technology. On that interpretation, such development is not guaranteed, even as a tendency, but it does suggest how there might be a generalization which could be tested against the findings of history. Note that this interpretation relies on the idea of *use*-fettering. If productive forces are already visible whose use would benefit subordinate groups, there is plausibility in the hypothesis that they will experience frustration and attempt to create circumstances where the forces can be used and the benefit received. There is less plausibility in hypothesizing that this will happen where such productive forces have not even been developed.

Marx employs the fettering metaphor and a related one in the case of the prospective transformation:

> Beyond a certain point, the development of the powers of production becomes a barrier for capital; hence the capital relation a barrier for the development of the productive powers of labour. When it has reached this point, capital, i.e. wage labour, enters into the same relation towards the development of social wealth and of the forces of production as the guild system, serfdom, slavery, and is necessarily stripped off as a fetter. (Marx, 1939: 749)

> The centralization of the means of production and the socialization of labour reach a point at which they become incompatible with their capitalist integument. This integument is burst asunder. The knell of

capitalist private property sounds. The expropriators are expropriated. (Marx, 1867a: 929)

Now if the fettering which Marx holds to be characteristic of capitalism fell into the general pattern distinguished under my interpretation, then (at least on a favourable outcome of the empirical evidence) this might provide a reason for thinking that the advent of the future society was probable, though not inevitable. It would be possible to appeal to an inductively grounded truth about what happens when the potential of new technology is frustrated by the fettering arising from inapposite social relations. However, I now suggest that there is a crucial difference in the nature of the fettering involved in Marx's account of capitalism. The upshot is that this inductive evidence is unavailable to him, with important consequences for his practical aspirations.

The imperative to maximize surplus-value ensures that capitalism both develops and uses productive forces at a startling rate. Marx, as we saw earlier, argues that the bourgeoisie cannot live without constantly revolutionizing the instruments of production (Marx and Engels, 1848: 70). Modern industry is revolutionary because 'it is continually transforming not only the technical basis of production but also the functions of the worker and the social combinations of the labour process' (Marx, 1867a: 617). Far from not using productive forces, the capitalist mode of production

begets, by its anarchic system of competition, the most outrageous squandering of labour-power and of the social means of production, not to mention the creation of a vast number of functions at present indispensable, but in themselves superfluous. (Marx, 1867a: 667; cf. *ibid.*: 618)

Presumably such squandering includes duplication of overheads, transportation, accounting, and so on, among competing units providing essentially the same goods and services, and use of resources for functions required by capitalism but otherwise not necessary for human welfare.

Should we conclude, therefore, that Marx's own analysis precludes the occurrence of fettering in capitalism? No. But the form of fettering it suffers from, on his account, is distinct from any of the interpretations of fettering previously considered. The productive forces are developed and used with abandon, but the imperatives of capitalism fetter their *rational* use. Resources could be deployed to create a humane environment. Instead, they receive 'a one-sided development only' and are 'for the majority destructive forces' (Marx and Engels, 1932: 76). This is illustrated by a discussion in *Capital* of the effects of the Factory Acts. Conceding that one such Act had improved health, Marx adds:

> At the same time, this part of the Act strikingly demonstrates that the capitalist mode of production, by its very nature, excludes all rational improvement beyond a certain point. (Marx, 1867a: 612)

He suggests that provision of working space and ventilation consistent with the health of workers would bankrupt thousands of small employers and in that way 'strike at the very roots of the capitalist mode of production' (*ibid.*). It is necessary for workers to have proper working space, and impossible to impose this rule on capital. Hence pulmonary diseases and the like 'are conditions necessary to the existence of capital' (*ibid.*). There is no technical difficulty in providing fresh air in the required volume, but what is technically possible may still be ruled out.

Fettering here is a qualitative rather than quantitative notion.[11] Use and development of productive forces continue, but are not guided directly by considerations of human need and welfare; they are guided by considerations of increase in surplus-value, with only incidental benefit to human beings. Fettering must be construed in a relative sense. The claim must be that capitalism dictates a less rational use than would be possible in some alternative system, rather than ceasing to allow any further rational use of resources at all.

Because the type of fettering changes between the diachronic materialism of Marx's general theory and the present context, his general theory (even if inductively established) cannot be used to support the idea that the prospective transformation is probable. Transcendence of fettering in his general theory requires action on the basis of the thought: 'These productive forces are not being used, and their not being used is not in the interests of a section of the population.' In the present case it would require action on the basis of the thought: 'These productive forces *are* being used, but their being used (in this way) is not in the interests of a section of the population.' To see something lying idle as a case of waste is different from seeing something in use as a case of waste. The latter requires different and more theoretically sophisticated responses.

It does not follow, of course, that Marx cannot establish that the transformation is probable, but he would have to provide further reasons for thinking so. And Marx himself is badly placed to argue, by appeal simply to rationality, that if resources are being squandered in a way that is disadvantageous to most members of society, they will eventually recognize this and act to rectify the situation. As he stresses, members of a society do not merely perceive their own social relations in a detached and neutral way, and capitalism in particular places problems in the path of a clear perception of its own processes. That is why they may seem natural. In the absence of any further argument from Marx, therefore, we must conclude that there is a dislocation between the material and the politico-psychological conditions for the transformation. He may have shown that capitalism has produced the productive forces which could be used to liberate most people from the onerous business of spending most of their waking hours in working to produce the means of life, but he has failed to show how this system itself produces the political consciousness required for deploying those resources to that end.

This conclusion may be less damaging than it appears. Marx's primary concern is not to establish a truth but to achieve a practical result: the introduction of the future society. He has failed to construct an argument with the conclusion that the introduction of the future society is probable. *But the point is to change that state of affairs.* The course for him to take, therefore, is to do whatever he thinks will make that eventuality more likely. He must do anything he can to challenge acceptance of capitalism as natural, everlasting and inescapable, and to promote commitment to its replacement. His own theory may be instrumental in that regard. If the absence of revolutionary consciousness is the major obstacle to the transformation, and if Marx has an effective diagnosis of the causes of that absence, then exposure to his diagnosis may be just what is required to render more probable that proposition which he was unable to infer as the conclusion of an argument.

To put the point in a less convoluted way: Marx's theories themselves commit him to taking seriously their own role as propaganda or, more neutrally, consciousness-raising.[12] This is not the same as his believing that 'men become good by reading books and listening to speeches . . . the purest idealism' (Nove, 1983: 17); nor should it attract the stigma of 'busily combing through the pages of *Theories of Surplus-Value* in search of social reality' (Parkin, 1979: ix). It merely reflects the characteristically Marxian belief that the theories to which people are exposed can themselves significantly influence their social perceptions, especially if the exposure occurs in propitious material circumstances.

Now we have seen that Marx looks askance at morality in general and class philanthropy in particular as a motivating force (4.4, 5.2). If the movement for transformation is not merely of the immense majority but also 'in the interest of the immense majority' (Marx and Engels, 1848: 78), then this wide band of people must be given *their own* reasons for acting. And it may seem out of the question that Marx should succeed in persuading a majority of the population that they have an escape-interest, an interest in abolishing their own status as a class, and thereby in mobilizing them for revolutionary purposes.

For one thing, Marx's social theory is 'unicentric': 'one group, form of oppression, struggle, or putatively deeper lying source of these things is said to constitute a unifying force which orders other phenomena' (Cunningham, 1987: 204). And the problem with this is that:

> nobody is just a worker. Each worker is also a person of a certain sex and sexual orientation, race, age, nationality, ethnicity, who has a certain state of health, who lives in a certain region and community, who is engaged in extraemployment activities such as those related to child rearing and recreating, and who has scales of values not all of which put advancing his or her interests as a worker at the top. (*ibid.*: 97)

With all these more particular interests, how could they be persuaded to adopt the favoured escape-interest as their overriding concern?

There is also the problem of 'transition costs': even if someone stands to gain by living in the future society, their working to achieve that result may put them into a worse situation in the interim than they currently occupy (cf. Wright, 1985: 288–91). A revolution has, 'even for most socialists, the character of an unlikely and risky leap into the dark' (Miller, 1984: 271). A dilemma then arises for any revolutionary organization: of needing to offer 'something now'. Without that, it cannot compete with organizations which have no such wider aspirations and can canvass support *solely* by appeal to what they can provide within the existing capitalist framework. The problem is that entering into this competition is liable to erode commitment to the revolutionary enterprise, as the securing of short-term gains assumes ever greater importance (cf. Przeworski, 1985: 8 ff., 240 ff.).

The strength of Marx's conception of class is that it will serve to pick out a large enough band of people to be capable of rebuilding society, and also that it is, so to speak, historically durable. It is a conception which is not outmoded by changes in the nature of work, or status, or the size of the gap between rich and poor. Its weakness is that the broad range of individuals which it picks out may be too large and diverse to act effectively in concert in the way demanded. It may be objected that the form of identification required by Marx's theories is simply unavailable, especially when we remember that he calls on the workers *of the world* to make a revolution. Elster argues that the cognitive conditions for recognizing class interests are hampered by the fact that basic class conflict may not be face-to-face. Workers may be separated from owners by a group of managers. 'Ultimate causal responsibility', he suggests, 'is less perceptible, and has less motivating power, than immediate confrontations' (Elster, 1985: 350). He concludes:

There are good philosophical, psychological and sociological grounds for thinking that individuals will always have a narrower focus of loyalty and solidarity than the international community of workers and capitalists. (*ibid.*: 397)

In a similar vein, Nove comments:

We can identify with a small group of people we know and can meet, with problems and effects we can actually observe; it is another matter if there are hundreds of millions of people, and multiple millions of decisions, great and small, with remote consequences which few can apprehend directly. (Nove, 1983: 19)

Even recognition of oneself as a member of the proletariat in Marx's sense requires an effort of abstraction: I must see myself not just as a welder or teacher or shop assistant; rather, I must abstract from these concrete considerations to the structural condition outlined in 4.2. Moreover, the implicit standard of comparison for ascribing class escape-interests is itself a hypothetical state of affairs. There is no existing state of affairs to which Marx can point in order to establish his claim, no system of common ownership where it can be *seen* that the interests of the working class are better served. If there were, Marx would not need to advocate the wholesale replacement of existing society.

These are all powerful criticisms. The only completely compelling rebuttal would be the actual occurrence of the transformation in accordance with Marx's prescription. In its absence, however, we should at least be aware of the full range of resources available to Marx from earlier discussion.

Though the criticisms proceed from an entirely natural view of revolution and what it entails, that view may not be apposite for present purposes. All that is conceptually involved in the idea of a revolution is fundamental change. As a matter of fact, revolutions have often involved immense hardship, cruelty and bloodshed. We saw in 5.2 a number of respects in which it would be necessary, according to Marx, for the prospective revolution to depart from earlier patterns, and this is germane to the present issue. If the prospective transformation requires the active collaboration of the majority, in conscious awareness of the project they are involved in and with a determination to complete it successfully, and if the existence and use of democratic institutions both facilitate such a change and confer legitimacy on it, then there is at least a raised probability that the transformation can take place with fewer negative features than earlier ones. Violence and dislocation may be minimized. That may at least reduce the power of one obstacle to the process, and it may set the scene for an alternative conception of revolutionary change which is not itself in the same way vastly dangerous and harsh. The impulsion to revolution might then be positive rather than negative: not desperation, the feeling that things could not be worse, but rather aspiration, the belief that there is much to be gained from the change.

Marx suggests that in one respect the transformation to the future society will be easier than that which brought capitalism into existence:

> The transformation of scattered private property resting on the personal labour of the individuals themselves into capitalist private property is naturally an incomparably more protracted, violent and difficult process than the transformation of capitalist private property, which in fact already rests on the carrying on of production by society, into social property. (Marx, 1867a: 929–30)

In other words, a massive upheaval was necessary to replace atomistic possession of productive resources with capitalist possession of much larger resources. But capitalist ownership became possible only through the collective, co-ordinated and concerted efforts of large numbers of people: the complex and valuable collective worker was born. What changes with the prospective transformation is simply the form of *ownership* of resources: this becomes social and universal, rather than individual or sectional. That change is minor compared with the drastic changes in people's conditions of life which were necessary for *production* to become social. There is no equivalent of the Enclosures Acts or the Highland Clearances as a precondition of converting productive assets, which are already collectively worked, into a common possession.

Marx's point is fair enough, but we should bear in mind that if ownership is equated with effective control, then massive changes are still involved in the transformation. The arguments of 5.1 and 5.2 should have shown clearly that the transformation of the collective worker from an unconscious to a conscious entity is itself a massive change. A self-willed change by large numbers of people from the position of subordinates to democratic participants in the social process is a further massive change, not a minor alteration to existing arrangements.

Recent discussions of whether Marx can give workers reasons for making a revolution have tended to proceed on the narrow assumptions about rationality identified and criticized in 2.6 (e.g. Buchanan, 1987: 114 ff.; Elster, 1985: 358–71; Przeworski, 1985: 171–203). Though Marx's position is indeed unicentric and, in the senses discussed earlier in this book, materialist, the motivational appeal he can rely on must not be narrowly construed. It is, so to speak, *multidirectional* both in substance and in form. In substance, he can appeal both to straightforwardly material considerations and to the relation between them and non-material considerations. In form, he can appeal both to individual and to collective aspirations. In these ways he can hope to speak to a variety of already-visible sources of motivation.

The simplest ground for the substance of his appeal may be thought to be material deprivation, yet this is in many ways the weakest. Someone suffering from it is likely to have a stronger reason for attempting, within existing relations, to acquire more material resources than for joining in revolutionary efforts. However, material welfare, narrowly defined, is not the only source of material interest, and it is consistent for Marx to rely on mobilization of concerns which extend beyond immediate material well-being (cf. Przeworski, 1985: 248). My aspiration may be to write poetry or worship my god, but since the fulfilment of virtually any reasonable aspirations itself requires different kinds of material resources, I thereby acquire an indirect material interest whose origin lies in a distinct, non-material circumstance. Paradoxically, this distances Marx's view from what we might call a crudely materialist conception of interests. Mere accumulation of wealth is in itself only one part of the picture.

Accordingly, it may be possible for Marx to appeal more generally to the projects which individuals cherish. He can argue that for their execution, unless they have reserves of wealth, they must make too great a sacrifice: forfeiture of a substantial portion of their life, in the expenditure of energy in forms over which they have relatively little control. Of course, one's life, projects and autonomy in the hours remaining after the work contract has been fulfilled may be enhanced as a result of entering into it, as compared simply with no such contract. But Marx will invite us to make a different comparison. In different, but realizable, circumstances the loss would be much less. In that endeavour, his appeal to the merely possible can be strengthened by appeal to actual circumstances: the prodigious achievements of capitalist technology continually provoke promises of an age of leisure and anxious discussions about people's ability to cope with it, yet that age never arrives.

Despite his unicentrism, Marx can agree that nobody is just a worker, and that people suffer oppression and acquire interests on the basis of other significant descriptions. He is not committed to disregarding, or treating as merely epiphenomenal, forms of oppression and interests distinct from those generated by the process of material exploitation. He need not regard, for example, religious or sexual oppression as really just a disguised form of class oppression. He is not even committed to regarding class oppression as *intrinsically* more important. He is committed to its centrality in other ways: its contingent centrality in our lives, given the kind of world we live in and the kind of creatures we are, in the ways outlined in his basic materialism; and its causal centrality in relation to many other forms of oppression, in the ways outlined in his synchronic materialism. Those centralities must hold in particular cases if his arguments are to have motivational appeal.

In discussions of unicentric and polycentric social theories, it is easy to proceed as if each type of oppression correlated with a different *group* of people. This is obviously not so, however. Clearly, blacks, women and workers are not separate groups of people. One individual may suffer none, some, most or even all of a given list of oppressions. A class appeal of the kind Marx must make is already an appeal to the great majority of people, and in this respect it differs from considerations such as gender, race or religion. But it involves persuading them to attend to their *overall* interest, rather than an interest arising from some particular description which applies to them. And such attention to overall interest, on Marx's view, leads back to his favoured class description.

The appeal to overall interests can be joined with an appeal based on the idea of coalition. Allow Marx all of the following as facts:

I hate my job, and indeed the whole business of having to work for someone for a wage or salary. You deplore the ravaging of the natural environment. Marx can show that the ravaging is the unavoidable result of a system based on wage labour, and that there is an alternative feasible system in which it would not occur. People with my views cannot join together with enough power to reach that alternative system; nor could people with your views. But in conjunction we all could.

In this model, though it might at first be thought that we do not share a common problem, on closer inspection it is reasonable to say that we do, or at the very least that we share a common *interest*. We have reason to join forces and utilize the potential common power we have for transforming social relations. The more Marx can establish connections of this kind between multifarious discontents and the capitalist system, the stronger the motivations he can appeal to. The abolition of the current form of class society may enable people with disparate objectives to achieve them, when anything less would not do so; or it may enable them to satisfy a whole range of interests. If multidirectional motivation can be established, then people who are hungry and people who want more time to play the clarinet can combine for their joint sakes, as long as they attend to their overall interests rather than interests arising from only one description which applies to them. Marx is not, therefore, confined to appealing to those whose discontent stems directly from their own position in the wage system; but the appeals he makes beyond this will rest on more ambitious theses he has embraced.

This picture is still incomplete if interests are represented as being exhausted in individual interests. I suggested in 2.5 that collective practical identification could also be a source of rational motivation, and that is of relevance to Marx. I may be motivated by collective goals such as the winning of a team game or the performance of a choral work, and I may regard my identity as so bound up with a collective to which I belong as to give me reasons for identifying with its own interests. In that spirit it may matter to me – and reasonably so – what happens to my species or, more significantly for Marx, to my class. The move from collective interest, in the sense merely of shared individual interests, to collective interest, in the sense of the interest of the collective itself, is just what is involved in the move from the working class being an invisible collective to becoming a self-conscious one. Workers share 'a common situation, common interests'; but when they constitute themselves into 'a class for itself' the interests the class defends 'become class interests' (Marx, 1847: 166).

There is an element in human thinking and behaviour which involves taking a broader view rather than focusing on immediate circumstances, drawing one's significance and one's motives from a wider arena than simply immediate gratification. In particular, there is an impulse to see one's significance as part of a larger whole. There is no reason why Marx should not tap into this, and connect aspirations arising from this broader view with material circumstances in his sense. If he can persuade at all, it will be on this terrain rather than that of short-term interests. He has little to offer people who want only 'something now', but people do not only or always want that. Sometimes they care deeply for the well-being of that of which they are merely a part.

Marx may be able to turn this issue to advantage by arguing that the very process of working for the transformation brings its own rewards. The political movement to initiate the transformation must foreshadow the future society, since qualities of competence in democratic decision-making must be fostered in advance if the future society is to function. That movement must therefore afford an arena where individual and collective autonomy are respected and promoted to a far greater extent than in other areas of life in the still-existing capitalist system. Far from being a cost, participation in the movement could then be seen as something to welcome: working in circumstances congenial to human development, in order to achieve what one regards as immensely worthwhile objectives.

Could people ever take a sufficiently long-term view, and sustain sufficiently wide identifications, to make their class escape-interests a priority? Marx can point to the wider identifications which people do already make, and press an analogy with wartime. In circumstances of war, people still have all their own particular interests arising from the multiplicity of descriptions which attach to them and the projects which they have embraced, and these interests continue to produce conflict both within and between them. But the threat of a common enemy is perceived as producing an overriding common interest in the enemy's defeat, an interest to which priority must be given. This shows that people in very disparate conditions may still recognize a common interest and act in a serious and committed way to pursue it. Just so, Marx will tell us, with capitalism (though the enemy for him is not the capitalist class but the capitalist *system*).

Marx's agenda is, by the standards of received political wisdom, extreme and bizarre, and his problems are undoubtedly compounded by the fact that he cannot galvanize people by pointing to any example of the sort of world he wishes to see. Indeed, when he is asked to show that that world is possible, he has to deflect the request back on to his questioners and insist that it is only they, not he, who are in a position to give such a demonstration. It is perhaps small wonder, then, that there has been no significant movement which at the same time identified itself according to Marx's criteria of class, embraced the objective specified by him and shared his views as to the prerequisites of carrying out the transformation.[13] Even if such a movement is neither inevitable nor probable but merely possible, however, it does not follow that it is irrational of Marx to attempt to foster it. The rationality of pursuing any objective depends not merely on the likelihood of success but on the product of that likelihood and the desirability of the outcome aimed at (cf. Parfit, 1984: 73–5). If massive gains would follow from the outcome, then even a small chance of success will justify the attempt. Hence, if Marx judges that the future society would involve a quantum leap for humanity, creating a world vastly superior to the present one in terms of the sort of life it made available for people, then, in the absence of compelling evidence that it is impossible, it makes sense for him to attempt to persuade us to turn our present world upside down. Whether it makes sense for us to listen depends on how much credence we place on the complicated network of argument with which he presents us.

Notes

1. Engels reiterates the importance of this commitment in his introduction to Marx's text (Engels, 1895: 121).
2. Marx also suggests that the need for such measures became outmoded, owing to giant strides in the development of productive forces (cf. Marx and Engels, 1872b: 21–2).

3. He does not necessarily *endorse* that idea. Cf. Chapter 4 n16.
4. Elster argues that in the 'Conspectus on Bakunin' Marx holds that the activities of future society will be non-conflictual, thereby relying unrealistically on unanimity and absence of divergent preferences (Elster, 1985: 457–8). However, what Marx envisages is the absence of *force* for resolving conflicts. Divergent preferences remain, and elections may be used for dealing with them, but 'election has nothing of its present political character' (Marx, 1874: 336), where politics is construed precisely as the expression of *class* conflict (*ibid.*; cf. Marx and Engels, 1848: 87; Marx, 1847: 167).
5. Marx's future society is certainly utopian in the literal sense of sharing features with More's *Utopia* – for example, the absence of exchange (More, 1516: 39, 45). But, unlike More's Utopia, it does not contain slaves (cf. *ibid.*: 44).
6. I have in mind proponents of 'non-market socialism' (cf. Rubel and Crump, 1987). The notion that Russia became a state-capitalist form of society has been associated more recently with quite different political tendencies, in particular some forms of Trotskyism, for which the question of when the degeneration occurred becomes important. For the non-market socialists there was never anything of the required kind to degenerate. Lenin himself had said that state-capitalism would be an advance for Russia, and as early as 1921 the German communist Otto Rühle characterized it in those terms (cf. Crump, 1987: 47; Shipway, 1987: 107).
7. Roemer might object that these explanations are not Marxist, since they 'take as an explanation of the phenomenon a description whose terms are political or sociological, rather than economic or materialist' (Roemer, 1982a: 5). However, we have seen that Marx's general theory allows a reciprocal influence between ideological and material factors (3.2). The explanation sketched here is not just that people may have got hold of Marxism as a theory and acted under the illusion that they were realizing its aspirations; it is that their doing so might be a very effective way of furthering material interests.
8. In the *Communist Manifesto* Marx describes 'the Communists' as 'the most advanced and resolute section of the working-class parties of every country' who 'have over the great mass of the proletariat the advantage of clearly understanding the line of march, the conditions, and the ultimate general results of the proletarian movement' (Marx and Engels, 1848: 79–80). This is the closest he ever comes to designating any agency as a vanguard. Even so, it is not the role of the communists to carry out the transformation. On the contrary, their aims include 'formation *of the proletariat* into a class' and 'conquest of political power *by the proletariat*' (*ibid.*; emphasis added).
9. In Britain, the Home Office Guidelines on the Work of a Special Branch, published in 1984, defined subversive activity as that intended to undermine or overthrow parliamentary democracy by political,

industrial or violent means. No doubt wholly negative and destructive acts, having nothing more than undermining as their objective, deserve that description; but it is not clear why peaceful political activity, aimed at replacing parliamentary by *more* democratic institutions, should be stigmatized in the same terms (cf. Graham, 1989b: 217).

10. Marx has reasons for thinking that capitalism has inherently self-destructive tendencies, such as the tendency of the rate of profit to fall. But the destruction of capitalism is not the same as the introduction of the future society, and we are investigating his reasons for thinking that the latter is likely.

11. This meets the ecopolitical complaint that Marx's views are outdated because he shares with the apologists of capitalism a belief in maximum growth and consumption. On the contrary, he is greatly concerned with the nature and quality of growth and consumption, as is also made clear in his observation that all progress in capitalist agriculture 'is a progress in the art, not only of robbing the worker, but of robbing the soil' (Marx, 1867a: 638).

12. Marx would not disagree. In 'Wage labour and capital' he refers to his 'wish to be understood by the workers' (Marx, 1849: 80). He regarded German workers' appreciation of *Capital* as 'the best reward for my labours' (Marx, 1873: 95), and applauded its serial publication in French, since 'the book will be more accessible to the working class, a consideration which to me outweighs everything else' (Marx, 1872: 104). He does warn in his preface to *Capital* that he assumes a reader 'willing to learn something new and therefore to think for himself' (Marx, 1867a: 90). He also assumes a reader who understands Greek and Latin, as well as several modern European languages (cf. Elster, 1985: 521).

13. Marx himself was hopeful that trade unions would play that role, and act as vehicles not only for the defence of workers' pay and conditions under capitalism but also for the abolition of the wages system and the emancipation of the proletariat (Marx, 1867b: 91; 1898: 447). Whatever the historical explanation for the failure of trade unions to play this dual role, it may be that the roles are so different that no organization *could* combine both functions.

Conclusion

At the heart of Marx's views is a conception of a different society, an attempt to establish the appropriateness of instituting that society in our own time, and an argument about the appropriate agency for achieving this. I have tried to indicate the complicated relations between these ideas and the more ambitious theses about the composition of society and the way in which to understand its historical progression, as well as the analysis of existing society. The latter proceeds at a deep structural level, and that is one reason why Marx's claims are of perennial, rather than merely historical, interest. The structural relations he is most interested in still obtain, and it is a complicated matter to determine how far and in what ways they are objectionable, either intrinsically or by virtue of their consequences.

If I am right in my claims, then, ironically, much Marxist tradition has misunderstood Marx and does face the threat of historical outdatedness. The concentration on manual labour has produced much narrower allegiances than Marx, on my interpretation, is committed to calling on. It also leaves no more than a vicarious concern in the rest of the population for the fate of a working class of which they form no part.

If Marx's ideas were formulated in the nineteenth century, the common assumption is that they were tested and found desperately wanting in the twentieth. The Eastern European experience, it may be said, shows how dangerous it is to abandon a known and imperfect world in search of an unknown and utopian one. The safety of step-by-step accretions of improvement has been amply vindicated.

It is true that Marx asks us to throw into doubt far more variables than most political theory does: the existence of the state, money, wage labour and the market are all called into question. However, I have tried to indicate that the route to the new society advocated by Marx himself is a moderate one. The preconditions for its realization are stringent, and involve amongst other things a transformation of consciousness without which the new society cannot possibly be realized. If I am right about this, then the failure of Eastern Europe can be read as a vindication of Marx's argument just as easily as a refutation. For that failure underlines the importance of his insistence on the need for appropriate preconditions, both in terms of mature material conditions and in terms of a mature, united and determined working class. It seems to me that in the long run it will be much easier to analyze and appraise Marx's programme without the distraction of a disastrously distorted model in the real world.

People who write philosophy books are in an exposed position because nothing can be taken for granted in philosophy, and any assumption can be challenged. Those who write books on Marx are exposed because of the sheer volume of his writings, and the even greater volume of interpretation. The exposure resulting from writing a philosophical book about Marx probably increases geometrically rather than arithmetically. I am aware that many of the positions which I have outlined are underdefended. Given the richness, complexity and interconnectedness of Marx's theories, their defence is not a task for one book or, indeed, one person. I have tried to contribute to an understanding of what his claims are, and to invest them with as much plausibility as possible (a principle of scholarship readily acceptable in other cases). But the enterprise of assessing Marx seems to me to be in its infancy. If his ideas were formulated in the nineteenth century and – to put it bluntly – dragged through the mud in the twentieth, the task of sober assessment may be something for the twenty-first century. Marx is our contemporary because we still have to clarify the statements he makes. They depend partly on normative questions and questions about human beings and their limits – matters about which it is much easier to have an opinion than to provide a good theory. We know too little about human nature and motivation to make swift and confident pronouncements in this area.

Given the corruption and distortion of Marx's ideas, it may be that whatever remains acceptable as post-Leninist Marxism can no longer be expressed in the language he used. George Orwell remarks somewhere that we sometimes have to decide whether a particular word is worth saving or not. In Marx's case it is a whole vocabulary whose salvage is in question. That raises the possibility that certain of his ideas might need to be re-expressed in new terminology, because of the deeply misleading associations which their expression has acquired. That, however, is a matter for future history.

Whatever the final assessment of Marx, my aspirations will be handsomely met if the reader is brought to give serious consideration to the arguments I have outlined. (Agreement would be going too far.) Even that requires a great act of imagination, and a preparedness to think beyond the parameters normally laid down. Marx invites us to relate to inanimate nature and to one another in a fundamentally different way. A prerequisite for this is that we conceive of our present relations very differently:

> The communist revolution is the most radical rupture with traditional property relations; no wonder that its development involves the most radical rupture with traditional ideas. (Marx and Engels, 1848: 86)

Bibliography

Works by Marx

Marx, K. (1846) Letter to P. V. Annenkov, reprinted in Marx (1847), 171–85.

Marx, K. (1847) *The Poverty of Philosophy*, 3rd impression, London, Lawrence and Wishart, n.d.

Marx, K. (1849) 'Wage labour and capital', in Marx and Engels (1962), vol. 1, 79–105.

Marx, K. (1850) *The Class Struggles in France*, in Fernbach (1973b), 35–142.

Marx, K. (1852a) 'The Chartists', *New York Daily Times*, 25 August, in Fernbach (1973b), 262–70.

Marx, K. (1852b) *The Eighteenth Brumaire of Louis Bonaparte*, in Fernbach (1973b), 143–249.

Marx, K. (1859) *A Contribution to the Critique of Political Economy*, London, Lawrence & Wishart, 1971.

Marx, K. (1864) 'Address and Provisional Rules of the International Working Men's Association', in Fernbach (1974), 73–84.

Marx, K. (1867a) *Capital*, vol. 1, Harmondsworth, Penguin, 1976.

Marx, K. (1867b) 'Instructions for delegates to the Geneva Congress', in Fernbach (1974), 85–93.

Marx, K. (1871) *The Civil War in France*, in Fernbach (1974), 187–268.

Marx, K. (1872) Preface to French edition of Marx (1867a), 24.

Marx, K. (1873) Postface to second edition of Marx (1867a), 94–103.

Marx, K. (1874) 'Conspectus on Bakunin', in Fernbach (1974), 333–8.

Marx, K. (1875) *Critique of the Gotha Programme*, in Fernbach (1974), 339–59.

Marx, K. (1877) Letter to the Editorial Board of *Otechestvenniye Zapiski*, in Feuer (1969), 476–9.

Marx, K. (1880) 'Introduction' to the Programme of the French Workers' Party, in Fernbach (1974), 376–7.

Marx, K. (1885) *Capital*, vol. 2, Harmondsworth, Penguin, 1978.

Marx, K. (1894) *Capital*, vol. 3, Harmondsworth, Penguin, 1981.

Marx, K. (1898) *Value, Price and Profit*, in Marx and Engels (1962), vol. 1 (under the title *Wages, Price and Profit*), 398–440.

Marx, K. (1905–10) *Theories of Surplus Value*, London, Lawrence & Wishart, 1969.

Marx, K. (1932) *Economic and Philosophic Manuscripts of 1844*, London, Lawrence & Wishart, 1961.

Marx, K. (1933) 'Results of the immediate process of production', in Marx (1867a), 949–1084.

Marx, K. (1939) *Grundrisse*, Harmondsworth, Penguin, 1973.

Works by Marx and Engels

Marx, K. and Engels, F (1845) *The Holy Family*, Moscow, Foreign Languages Publishing House, 1956.

Marx, K. and Engels, F. (1848) *Manifesto of the Communist Party*, in Fernbach (1973a), 67–98.

Marx, K. and Engels, F. (1871) *Resolutions of the Conference of Delegates of the International Working Men's Association*, in Fernbach (1974), 269–70.

Marx, K. and Engels, F. (1872a) 'The alleged splits in the International', in Fernbach (1974), 272–313.

Marx, K. and Engels, F. (1872b) Preface to *Manifesto of the Communist Party*, 1872 German edn, in Marx and Engels (1962), vol. 1, 21–2.

Marx, K. and Engels, F. (1879) Circular letter to Bebel, Liebknecht, Bracke *et al.*, in Fernbach (1974), 360–75.

Marx, K. and Engels, F. (1882) Preface to *Manifesto of the Communist Party*, 1882 Russian edn, in Marx and Engels (1962), vol. 1, 22–4.

Marx, K. and Engels, F. (1885) 'Address of the Central Committee to the Communist League', in Marx and Engels (1962), vol. 1, 106–17.

Marx, K. and Engels, F. (1932) *The German Ideology*, London, Lawrence & Wishart, 1965.

Works by Engels

Engels, F. (1883) Speech at the Graveside of Karl Marx, *Sozialdemokrat*, 22 March, in Marx and Engels (1962), vol. 2, 167–9.

Engels, F. (1888) Preface to 1888 English edn of Marx and Engels (1848), in Fernbach (1973a), 162–6.

Engels, F. (1891) Introduction to Marx (1871), in Marx and Engels (1962), vol. 1, 471–85.

Engels, F. (1895) Introduction to Marx (1850), in Marx and Engels (1962), vol. 1, 118–39.

Collections

Fernbach, D. (ed.) (1973a) *The Revolutions of 1848*, Harmondsworth, Penguin.
Fernbach, D. (ed.) (1973b) *Surveys from Exile*, Harmondsworth, Penguin.
Fernbach, D. (ed.) (1974) *The First International and After*, Harmondsworth, Penguin.
Feuer, L. S. (ed.) (1969) *Marx and Engels: Basic writings on politics and philosophy*, Glasgow, Collins.
Marx, K. and Engels, F. (1962) *Marx and Engels: Selected writings*, 2 vols, London, Lawrence & Wishart.

Other Works Cited

Acton, H. B. (1962) *The Illusion of the Epoch*, 2nd impression, London, Routledge & Kegan Paul.
Andrew, E. (1983) 'Class in itself and class against capital: Karl Marx and his classifiers', *Canadian Journal of Political Science*, vol. 16, 577–84.
Arneson, R. (1981) 'What's wrong with exploitation?', *Ethics*, vol. 91, 202–27.
Arnold, N. S. (1987) 'Recent work on Marx: A critical survey', *American Philosophical Quarterly*, vol. 24, 277–93.
Ball, T. and Farr, J. (eds) (1984) *After Marx*, Cambridge, Cambridge University Press.
Böhm-Bawerk, E. (1896) *Karl Marx and the Close of his System*, ed. Sweezy, P., London, Merlin Press, 1975.
Braybrooke, D. (1987) *Meeting Needs*, Princeton, NJ, Princeton University Press.
Brenner, R. (1976) 'Agrarian class structure and economic development in pre-industrial Europe', *Past & Present*, vol. 70, 30–70.
Bricianer, S. (1978) *Pannekoek and the Workers' Councils*, St Louis, MO, Telos Press.
Buchanan, A. (1982) *Marx and Justice*, London, Methuen.
Buchanan, A. (1987) 'Marx, morality and history', *Ethics*, vol. 98, 104–36.
Carling, A. (1986) 'Rational choice Marxism', *New Left Review*, no. 160, 24–62.
Cohen, G. A. (1970) 'On some criticisms of historical materialism', *Supplementary Proceedings of the Aristotelian Society*, vol. 44, 121–42.
Cohen, G. A. (1978) *Karl Marx's Theory of History*, Oxford, Clarendon Press.
Cohen, G. A. (1980) 'Reply to Elster', *Political Studies*, vol. 28, 129–35.

Cohen, G. A. (1982) 'Reply to Elster on Marxism, functionalism and game theory', *Theory and Society*, vol. 11, 483–96.

Cohen, G. A. (1986) 'The structure of proletarian unfreedom' in Roemer (ed.) (1986), 237–59.

Cohen, G. A. (1988) *History, Labour and Freedom*, Oxford, Clarendon Press.

Cohen, G. A. (1990a) 'Marxism and contemporary political philosophy, or why Nozick exercises some Marxists more than he does any egalitarian liberals', *Canadian Journal of Philosophy*, supplementary vol. 16, 363–87.

Cohen, G. A. (1990b) 'Self-ownership, communism and equality', *Supplementary Proceedings of the Aristotelian Society*, vol. 64, 25–44.

Cohen, J. (1982) 'Review of G. A. Cohen's *Karl Marx's Theory of History*', *Journal of Philosophy*, vol. 79, 253–73.

Cohen, M., Nagel, T. and Scanlon, T. (eds) (1980) *Marx, Justice and History*, Princeton, NJ, Princeton University Press.

Crump, J. (1987) 'The thin red line: Non-market socialism in the twentieth century', in Rubel and Crump (eds) (1987), 35–59.

Cunningham, F. (1987) *Democratic Theory and Socialism*, Cambridge, Cambridge University Press.

Draper, H. (1986) *Karl Marx's Theory of Revolution*, vol. 3, New York, Monthly Review Press.

Draper, H. (1987) *The 'Dictatorship of the Proletariat' from Marx to Lenin*, New York, Monthly Review Press.

Elster, J. (1979) *Ulysses and the Sirens*, Cambridge, Cambridge University Press.

Elster, J. (1980) 'Review of G. A. Cohen's *Karl Marx's Theory of History*', *Political Studies*, vol. 28, 121–8.

Elster, J. (1982) 'Marxism, functionalism and game theory', *Theory and Society*, vol. 11, 453–82.

Elster, J. (1985) *Making Sense of Marx*, Cambridge, Cambridge University Press.

Elster, J. (ed.) (1986a) *Rational Choice*, Oxford, Blackwell.

Elster, J. (1986b) 'Three challenges to class' in Roemer (ed.) (1986), 141–61.

Evans, M. (1975) *Karl Marx*, London, Allen & Unwin.

Gellner, E. (1980) 'A Russian Marxist philosophy of history' in Gellner, E. (ed.) *Soviet and Western Anthropology*, London, Duckworth, 59–82.

Geras, N. (1983) *Marx and Human Nature: Refutation of a legend*, London, Verso.

Geras, N. (1985) 'The controversy about Marx and justice', *New Left Review*, no. 150, 47–85.

Gough, I. (1972) 'Marx's theory of productive and unproductive labour', *New Left Review*, no. 76, 47–72.

Graham, K. (1981) 'Illocution and ideology', in Mepham, J. and Ruben, D.-H. (eds) *Issues in Marxist Philosophy*, vol. 4, Sussex, Harvester, 153–94.

Graham, K. (1986a) *The Battle of Democracy*, Sussex, Wheatsheaf.

Graham, K. (1986b) 'Morality and abstract individualism', *Proceedings of the Aristotelian Society*, vol. 87, 21–33.

Graham, K. (1987) 'Morality, individuals and collectives' in Evans, J. D. G. (ed.) *Moral Philosophy and Contemporary Problems*, Cambridge, Cambridge University Press, 1–18.

Graham, K. (1989a) 'Class – a simple view', *Inquiry*, vol. 32, 419–36.

Graham, K. (1989b) 'Freedom, liberalism and subversion', in Hoggart, R. (ed.) *Liberty and Legislation*, London, Frank Cass, 205–22.

Graham, K. (1990) 'Self-ownership, communism and equality', *Supplementary Proceedings of the Aristotelian Society*, vol. 64, 45–61.

Hollis, M. (1987) *The Cunning of Reason*, Cambridge, Cambridge University Press.

Jordan, B. (1989) *The Common Good*, Oxford, Blackwell.

Lenin, V. I. (1902) *What is to be Done?*, Moscow, Progress Publishers, 1978.

Lenin, V. I. (1918) *The State and Revolution*, Peking, Foreign Languages Press, 1976.

Lenin, V. I. (1920) *'Left-Wing' Communism, an Infantile Disorder*, Moscow, Progress Publishers, 1975.

Levine, A., Sober, E. and Wright, E. O. (1987) 'Marxism and methodological individualism', *New Left Review*, no. 162, 67–84.

Levine, A. and Wright, E. O. (1980) 'Rationality and class struggle', *New Left Review*, no. 123, 47–68.

Little, D. (1989) 'Marxism and popular politics' in Ware and Nielsen (eds) (1989), 163–204.

Lukes, S. (1983) 'Can the base be distinguished from the superstructure?', in Miller, D. and Siedentop, L. (eds) *The Nature of Political Theory*, Oxford, Clarendon Press, 103–20.

Lukes, S. (1985) *Marxism and Morality*, Oxford, Clarendon Press.

McLellan, D. (1971) *The Thought of Karl Marx*, London, Macmillan.

McLellan, D. (1973) *Karl Marx: His life and thought*, London, Macmillan.

McMurtry, J. (1978) *The Structure of Marx's World View*, Princeton, NJ, Princeton University Press.

Mandel, E. (1978) 'Introduction' to Marx (1885), 11–79.

Miliband, R. (1977) *Marxism and Politics*, Oxford, Oxford University Press.

Miller, R. (1975) 'The consistency of historical materialism', *Philosophy and Public Affairs*, vol. 4, reprinted in Cohen, M. *et al.* (eds) (1980), 235–54.

Miller, R. (1984) *Analyzing Marx*, Princeton, NJ, Princeton University Press.

Mills, C. W. (1985) ' "Ideology" in Marx and Engels', *Philosophical Forum*, vol. 16, 327–46.

Moore, S. (1975) 'Marx and Lenin as historical materialists', *Philosophy and Public Affairs*, vol. 4, reprinted in Cohen, M. *et al.* (eds) (1980), 211–34.

More, T. (1516) *Utopia*, ed. Logan, G. and Adams, R., Cambridge, Cambridge University Press, 1989.

Nagel, T. (1986) *The View from Nowhere*, Oxford, Oxford University Press.

Nicolaus, M. (1967) 'Proletariat and middle class in Marx', *Studies on the Left*, vol. 7, 22–49.

Nove, A. (1983) *The Economics of Feasible Socialism*, London, Allen & Unwin.

Nozick, R. (1974) *Anarchy, State, and Utopia*, New York, Basic Books.

O'Neill, O. (1986) *Faces of Hunger*, London, Allen & Unwin.

Pannekoek, A. (1921) 'Soviet Russia and Western European Communism', *De Nieuwe Tijd*, 436–48, in Bricianer (1978).

Pannekoek, A. (1938) *Lenin as Philosopher*, London, Merlin Press, 1975.

Parfit, D. (1984) *Reasons and Persons*, Oxford, Clarendon Press.

Parkin, F. (1979) *Marxism and Class Theory*, London, Tavistock.

Plamenatz, J. (1963) *Man and Society*, vol. 2, London, Longmans.

Popper, K. (1957) *The Poverty of Historicism*, 2nd edn, London, Routledge, 1963.

Poulantzas, N. (1975) *Classes in Contemporary Capitalism*, London, New Left Books.

Przeworski, A. (1985) *Capitalism and Social Democracy*, Cambridge, Cambridge University Press.

Reiman, J. (1989) 'An alternative to "distributive" Marxism', in Ware and Nielsen (eds) (1989), 299–332.

Roemer, J. (1982a) *A General Theory of Exploitation and Class*, Cambridge, MA, Harvard University Press.

Roemer, J. (1982b) 'New directions in the Marxian theory of exploitation and class', *Politics and Society*, vol. 11, reprinted in Roemer (ed.) (1986), 81–113.

Roemer, J. (ed.) (1986) *Analytical Marxism*, Cambridge, Cambridge University Press.

Roemer, J. (1989) 'Second thoughts on property relations and exploitation', in Ware and Nielsen (eds) (1989), 257–66.

Rubel, M. and Crump, J. (eds) (1987) *Non-Market Socialism in the Nineteenth and Twentieth Centuries*, London, Macmillan.

Schumpeter, J. (1943) *Capitalism, Socialism and Democracy*, 4th edn, London, Unwin, 1954.

Shaw, W. H. (1978) *Marx's Theory of History*, London, Hutchinson.

Shaw, W. H. (1989) 'Ruling ideas', in Ware and Nielsen (eds) (1989), 425–48.

Shipway, M. (1987) 'Council communism', in Rubel and Crump (eds) (1987), 104–26.

Steedman, I. (ed.) (1981) *The Value Controversy*, London, Verso.

Taylor, M. (1986) 'Elster's Marx', *Inquiry*, vol. 29, 3–10.

Tully, J. and Skinner, Q. (1988) *Meaning and Context*, Princeton, NJ, Princeton University Press.

Van Parijs, P. (1981) *Evolutionary Explanation in the Social Sciences*, New Jersey, Rowman & Littlefield.

Van Parijs, P. (1982) 'Functionalist Marxism rehabilitated', *Theory and Society*, vol. 11, 497–511.

Van Parijs, P. (1984) 'Marxism's central puzzle', in Ball and Farr (eds) (1984), 88–104.

Van Parijs, P. (1989) 'In defence of abundance', in Ware and Nielsen (eds) (1989), 467–96.

Ware, R. and Nielsen, K. (eds) (1989) *Analyzing Marxism*, Calgary, AB, University of Calgary Press.

Williams, B. (1985) *Ethics and the Limits of Philosophy*, London, Fontana.

Wolff, R. P. (1981) 'A critique and reinterpretation of Marx's labour theory of value', *Philosophy and Public Affairs*, vol. 10, 89–120.

Wolff, R. P. (1984) *Understanding Marx*, Princeton, NJ, Princeton University Press.

Wood, A. (1981) *Karl Marx*, London, Routledge & Kegan Paul.

Wood, A. (1984) 'Justice and class interests', *Philosophica*, vol. 33, 9–32.

Wood, A. (1986) 'Historical materialism and functional explanation', *Inquiry*, vol. 29, 11–27.

Wright, E. O. (1985) *Classes*, London, Verso.

Wright, E. O. (1986) 'What is middle about the middle class?', in Roemer (ed.) (1986), 114–40.

Name Index

Subject Index